BASICS
ARCHITECTURE

Nicola Crowson

Representational Techniques for Architecture

Second Edition

Fairchild Books
An imprint of Bloomsbury Publishing PLC

Fairchild Books
An imprint of Bloomsbury Publishing Plc

Imprint previously known as AVA Publishing

50 Bedford Square   1385 Broadway
London   New York
WC1B 3DP   NY 10018
UK   USA
www.bloomsbury.com

FAIRCHILD BOOKS, BLOOMSBURY and the Diana logo
are trademarks of Bloomsbury Publishing Plc

First published 2007
© Bloomsbury Publishing Plc, 2015

British Library Cataloguing-in-Publication Data
A catalogue record for this book is available from the
British Library.

ISBN: PB: 978-1-4725-2785-1
ePDF: 978-1-4725-2976-3

Library of Congress Cataloging-in-Publication Data
Farrelly, Lorraine.
Representational techniques for architecture / Lorraine
Farrelly, Nicola
Crowson. – Second edition.
    pages cm – (Basics architecture)
"First published 2007."
Includes bibliographical references and index.
ISBN 978-1-4725-2785-1 (paperback)
1. Architectural drawing. 2. Architectural drawing–
Computer-aided design. I. Crowson, Nicola. II. Title.
NA2700.F37 2014
720.28'4–dc23
                    2014030471

Layout by Jane Harper
www.harperandcole.co.uk
Printed and bound in China

0.1

**Project: Master plan sketch for
the new World Trade Center
Location: New York, USA
Architect: Studio Daniel
Libeskind**

This sketch uses techniques of
sketch and perspective drawing.
The perspective is imagined from
above giving priority to the memorial
landscape edges by the tower
blocks. The pen sketch uses a
beautiful line quality, which suggests
high-rise buildings and landscape
features. Colored pencil has been
added to the sky and the memorial
within the landscape.

0.1

Contents

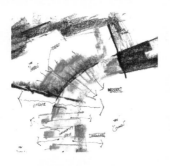  

  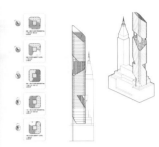

Introduction

Representation is an important aspect of any visual or design-based discipline. In architecture, the ideas that are expressed through drawings and models may eventually become buildings. This book explores the techniques that are used to represent architectural and interior spaces, buildings and places. These forms of representation are constantly changing and are informed by techniques used in other design disciplines. The relationship between freehand drawing and computer-generated images is evolving, and designers can now combine these forms of representation to show their concepts. The theoretical ideas associated with architectural drawing have been developed from Renaissance traditions; and these concepts of perspective drawing are still used today whether in freehand or computer-aided design (CAD) images.

This second edition builds on ideas introduced in the first edition. It includes new case studies from architects from around the world; these are used to illustrate the techniques described in the book. At the end of every section, there are new projects for students to encourage them to apply what they have learned in the chapter. Updated images show how to draw and illustrate architectural ideas. In addition, the section on digital technology has been increased to include information about BIM —Building Information Modeling.

To move through this process of architectural design requires a variety of skills. Freehand, loose or intuitive drawings and models are employed when concept and abstraction are critical factors; they can encourage freedom of thought and expression. As the architectural design develops, the precise detail of CAD drawings might be necessary to explore aspects of a building in terms of construction or manufacture. A competent architect needs to have a range of skills to generate the right type of image to suit the given stage in the design process. The quick freehand drawing may be the start of a process that builds to a complex set of three-dimensional (3D) drawings and CAD models. There are evolving approaches to architectural representation associated with computer software. BIM is a way to create 3D computer models in detail before the building starts on-site. This system allows a building to be managed more efficiently during the construction process. Using BIM means that there is a digital online portfolio of drawings as well as a live virtual model.

Architectural drawings use a varied language; the vocabulary is basic. Architects understand this language; it can be a simple communication, such as a freehand drawing, or complex, such as construction details and sections through buildings that communicate information about materials, structures and dimensions. Ideas are expressed as lines, and all lines or strokes on a page are careful and considered. Each project will use the language differently; this will depend on the size, scale and the construction techniques and processes involved in the building of the project. Many architectural schemes literally stay on the drawing board and do not get to the stage of building but remain as ideas or intentions.

As with all drawing techniques, it is important to practice and develop your own skills, and to try new approaches, so that you can adapt your individual methods to different situations.

This book has been designed to identify a series of different aspects of drawing from sketch to presentation. Each section has many visual examples and precedents of drawing along with a project for students so that they can explore the ideas. In addition, each chapter has a case study from an architect's practice to illustrate ideas in the book and to show how these drawing ideas work in practice.

Sketch

This section explores ideas of how to sketch and draw at all stages of the design process. The new case study and project pages introduce you to design sketches and how to create a city sketchbook.

Scale

This section looks at the range of specific drawing scales that can be used at various stages of the architectural design process. Understanding the application of these scales for different situations is critical. The new case study and project pages introduce you to how to use scale and how to undertake a measured survey.

Orthographic projection

Orthographic projection looks at the measured drawings that explain the idea of the building in two-dimensional (2D) form: plans, sections and elevations. These 2D drawings reveal the 3D intention of the building. The new case study and project pages introduce you to orthographic drawings from an architectural practice and explore render plans and section drawings.

3D images

3D images are easily accessible and provide a perspective view of a space, which will give an impression of the experience of the building on a particular site or location. 3D images are also useful for creating construction and assembly drawings. The new case study and project pages will introduce you to collage in relation to 3D drawings and explore perspective sketches.

Modeling

Modeling ideas allow an exploration spatially of concepts, spaces and form at all stages of the design process. Models can be created physically or by using CAD software. The new case study and project pages will introduce you to physical and CAD modeling in practice and demonstrate how to make city models.

Layout and presentation

The communication of the idea is critical. How it is organized and presented is an important design consideration. The new case study and project pages will introduce you to presentation drawings used in practice and demonstrate how to structure portfolios.

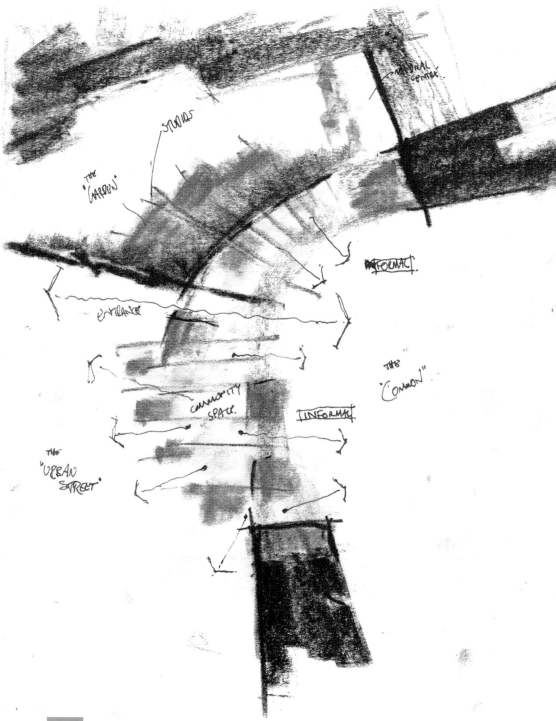

MEDICAL CENTER

STAIRS

"THE GARDEN"

FORMAL

ENTRANCE

THE "COMMON"

COMMUNITY SPACE.

INFORMAL

THE "URBAN STREET"

1 Sketch

A sketch needs to be quick, loose and open. It is the speed inherent in this sort of drawing that makes it a powerful way to describe an idea. Forms of sketching can range from visual note-taking, observing real conditions and situations, to the production of analytical drawings that deconstruct an idea or concept. Sketches can be categorized according to concept, analysis and observation.

Conceptual sketches can reveal the essence of a complex idea. The challenge in the concept sketch is to clearly and concisely communicate the design intention. A concept sketch may be drawn at the beginning of the project, and it should still be relevant on the project's completion.

Analytical sketches can be used to analyze a building, space or component. These can be created at any stage of the design process. In a project's initial stages they may convey a design intention; later on in the design process they can explain ideas associated with journeys through the building or aspects of construction.

Observational sketches can be used to describe aspects of buildings, exploring materials or space in detail. This type of drawing is about careful consideration of a view, exploring an aspect of a space or place and taking time to record it.

There are many sketching techniques that can be explored and further developed until individual preferences and a personal style are established. A personal sketching technique needs to be developed through practice and experimentation. Carry a sketchbook with you so that you can record ideas, and work through concepts—it's an extension of memory. Practice will improve observation and drawing skill.

1.1

Project: Conceptual proposal for a health living center
Location: Leigh Park, Hampshire, UK
Designer: Jonny Sage

This charcoal sketch shows the conceptual relationship between an idea for a building and how it connects to the surrounding landscape.
The heaviness of the charcoal lines represents the solidity of the building forms and the accents of blue represent pools of water.

Tools and materials

Sketching requires a range of tools, and first and foremost is the sketchbook itself. When selecting a sketchbook, important factors to consider are convenience, portability, and the purpose of your intended drawings. It's also important to purchase the best quality paper you can afford. Better quality paper will be more flexible as it will work equally well if sketching in pencil or pen, or if using watercolors.

An A4 (210 x 297 mm or 8.3 x 11.7 inches) sketchbook is a good starting point, as the page is large enough to accommodate experimentation with different sketching techniques, and it allows bigger images to be produced. Alternatively, an A5 (148 x 210 mm or 5.8 x 8.3 inches) sketchbook is very useful for travel because it fits neatly into a pocket and can be carried easily. An A3 (297 x 420 mm or 11.7 x 16.5 inches) sketchbook is excellent for life and large-scale observational drawings (such as elevations).

1.2

Project: Living Bridge proposal
Location: Aalborg, Denmark
Designer: Joshua Kievenaar

This perspective sketch depicts a view across a bridge towards the city of Aalborg, Denmark. It uses mixed media to suggest the quality of the materials of the bridge, water, and sky. The perspective and white foreground draw the eye to the center of the image and to the city skyline in the distance.

Line hierarchy

When sketching, it is an excellent idea to have a range of pens, pencils, and coloring media at your disposal because the thickness of the lines in a sketch are extremely important. There is a hierarchy associated with the line, and its values vary in sketching. A fine line can be used for shading and detail, and a thicker, heavier line will suggest form and substance.

Different drawing media will affect the line hierarchy. Fiber-tip pens, which are available in a range of nib sizes, are useful for capturing detail. Pencils can also supply a range of line weights as well as being available in soft (B) and hard (H) leads. Using varied pencil types will allow a range of differently styled sketches to be developed. A 0.5 mm propelling pencil, with a range of hard and soft leads, is another versatile drawing tool.

Sketching with a black-ink pen is an important skill to develop because the contrast that the ink line produces against the paper, and the permanence of the line, results in a definite image.

One tool that is probably unnecessary is an eraser. When sketching, practice is very important and even the mistakes can be important lessons, so it makes sense not to rub them out. Remember, a sketchbook is a collection of drawings, and it reflects the development of techniques and ideas. It is also about developing confidence and seeing the progress in drawing technique.

1.2

Tools for architectural drawing

To enjoy sketching, and achieve a range of results, it is important to have different sorts of equipment to experiment with. Simple drawings can be produced with a single sheet of paper and a pencil. Then, by further considering the type of pencil and the type of paper, the possible variations are endless. With each drawing, experiment with a new tool or medium. Listed here is a range of equipment that can help you vary and further your drawing experiences.

- Mechanical pencils (0.3 or 0.5 mm)
- Fiber-tip pens (0.2, 0.5, 0.8 mm)
- Adjustable set square
  (20 cm or 8 x 8 inches)
- 45-degree set square
- 60-degree set square
- Circle template
- Architect's scale rule
  (30 cm or 12 inches)
- Roll of white tracing paper
- Roll of sketch and trace/detail paper
- A3 (297 x 420 mm or 11.7 x 16.5 inches)
  tracing paper block (60 gsm or 40.5 lbs)
- Drawing board
- Sketchbook
- Tape measure
- Set of French curves

Conceptual sketches

Architectural ideas or concepts are described in a form of sketch shorthand. A conceptual explanation of how a building works can sometimes be conveyed in a simple line drawing. Conversely, the concept may be more complex and so require a series of sketches to fully explain the underlying idea.

A concept can be related to any aspect of the architectural design process. For example, an urban concept might reference the scale of a city or location, or a material concept could describe the different details of a building and how they are connected together. The architectural concept can be conveyed in both the macro and micro elements of a scheme design.

At any stage of the process, the concept is something that drives the design forward and as such it needs to be recorded. A sketch is a quick, easy, and useful way to do this, and a concept sketch can take many forms.

1.3

Project: Oxford Brookes
University Campus
Location: Oxford, UK
Architect: Design Engine

A parti drawing is reductive; it displays a complex idea in a very simple form. This concept parti drawing reduces the concept of a university building to a diagram. The design idea is concerned with how building elements insert a double-height atrium space.

1.4

Project: The Visitor Centre,
Hardwick Park
Location: Durham, UK
Architect: Design Engine

These images describe the construction process for a project that consists of large prefabricated elements that will be transported to the site and bolted together. The drawing is a perspective sketch to explain the removal of the elements from a truck and how they will be located and assembled on a hard-to-access site.

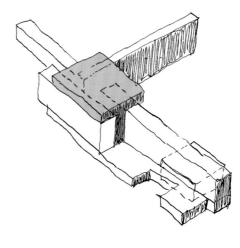

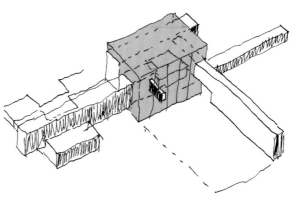

1.3

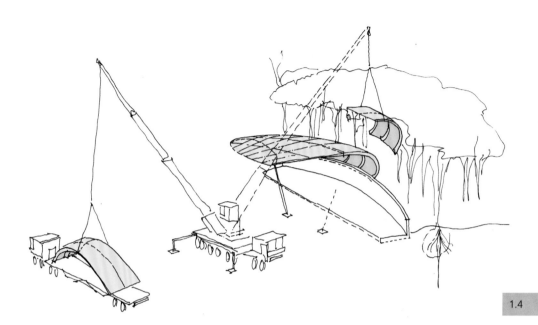

1.4

Parti diagrams

Concepts are dynamic, and the clearest forms of conceptual design will be simple and informative. A parti diagram (the term is derived from the French verb *prendre parti,* which means to make a choice) is very helpful in this respect. Popularized during the nineteenth century in the École des Beaux-Arts in Paris, France, these drawings are reductive and transform the concept into a few simple lines, which explain complex ideas and motifs in clear and simple terms. Parti diagrams are abstract sketches that are loaded with architectural meaning and intent, and can be referred to at all stages of the design project.

Reductive parti drawings are simple in their execution, but require a great deal of consideration as they are often underpinned by quite complex thought processes. As such, they convey a meaning that goes beyond the line on the paper and will usually need to be fully described by accompanying text.

The concept sketch may also require descriptive text or commentary alongside the drawing in order to strongly associate the drawing with its architectural intention.

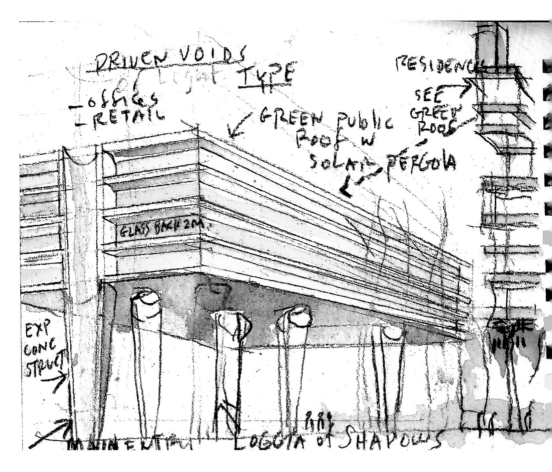

1.5

Project: Dongguan master plan
Location: Dongguan, China
Architect: Steven Holl Architects

These sketches use elevation
and perspective to analyze and
reflect on the key design ideas
of blocks in the landscape.
Colored accents highlight the
horizontal layers of the towers
and indicate green spaces. The
sketches are drawn in soft pencil
with accents of watercolor.

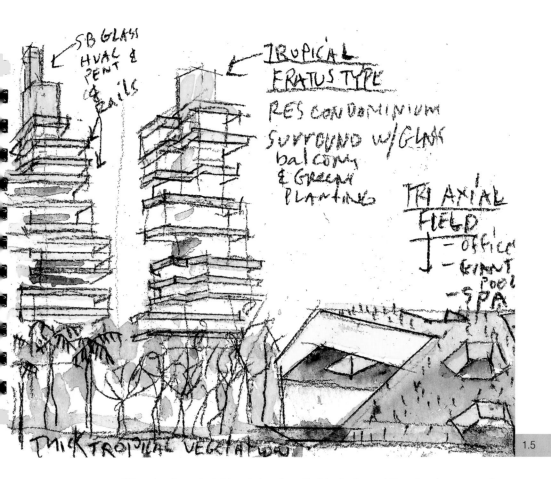

1.5

"Drawing in a sketchbook teaches first to look, and then to observe and finally perhaps to discover …. and it is then that inspiration might come."
Le Corbusier

Analytical sketches

Analysis of an idea requires a way of thinking that separates, simplifies, and clarifies. An analytical sketch usually follows the same working principles and as such is a device that can help explain complex aspects of architecture.

Analytical drawings can be used to isolate specific aspects of an architectural idea and describe them as a series of parts or components. So, analytical drawings could be used technically to describe the structural system of a building, or equally take an environmental approach and describe how sunlight moves through a space, or they may even describe a building's construction or assembly system. When designing building systems, architects will use analytical sketches to work through their ideas and develop particular responses that will shape their overall design approach.

The analysis of an idea needs to be logical and easy to understand. The drawings that first begin the process of an architectural design are site analysis sketches. Whether these analyze a building, an urban site or a landscape, these drawings describe what already exists—whether it is an aspect of the local environmental conditions, or the type of materials used on the site, or a reference to a previous event—as a series of critical diagrams. These analytical diagrams separate ideas that will inform and influence the subsequent architectural design.

Using analytical sketches to record site information produces a map of the site's building forms, histories and its topography, which combine to create a full picture of the site conditions. They will reference aspects of the site that can be described "as is", in the present, and "as was", in the past. Analytical sketches are effectively a form of on-site note-taking.

1.6

Project: The Paddocks
Location: Brockenhurst, UK
Architect: PAD Studio

These drawings use plan, section and 3D sketches to explore the remodeling of The Paddocks in the village of Brockenhurst. They illustrate design ideas in relation to site conditions and building form.

The exploded isometric sketch uses diagramming to explain the concept. Color has been added to highlight key information such as circulation, living, and external space.

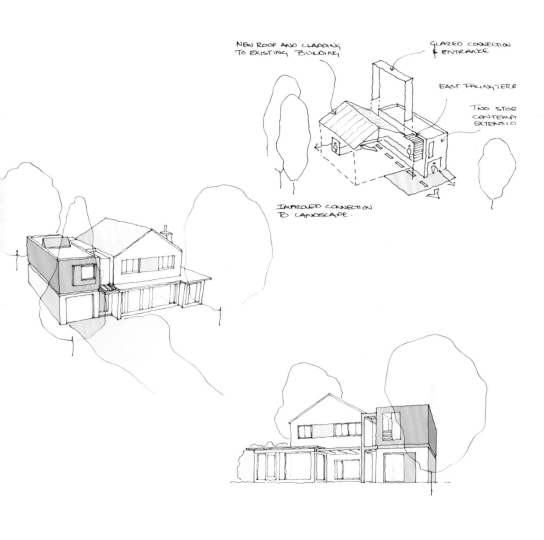

NEW ROOF AND CLADDING
TO EXISTING BUILDING

GLAZED CONNECTION
& ENTRANCE

EAST FACING TERR

TWO STOR
CONTEMPL
EXTENSIO

IMPROVED CONNECTION
TO LANDSCAPE.

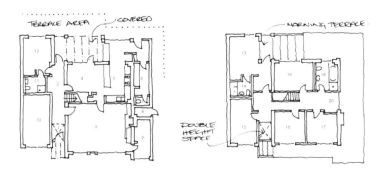

TERRACE AREA   COVERED

MORNING TERRACE

DOUBLE
HEIGHT
SPACE

1.6

Conceptual field

As well as being used at the beginning of the design process, as the scheme of a building further develops, many of the architectural drawings produced are analytical (even the detail drawings that explain the assembly of a building are themselves a form of analysis).

For example, analytical sketches can be used to explain site interpretation, any structural and environmental ideas for the site, and detailed construction and assembly ideas. Cities can also be described through analytical drawing or mapping, and doing so often reduces complex forms of urban design to simple diagrams and sketches.

A series of analytical sketches will describe the thinking and evolution of the design idea, deconstructing it into stages of development and understanding. These sketches will reveal the thinking of the architect or designer and how it has influenced the final architectural scheme.

1.7
___

Project: The National Portrait Gallery
Location: London, UK
Architect: Dixon Jones

This drawing shows a proposed relationship between Trafalgar Square, The National Gallery and The National Portrait Gallery. It was intended to create a new view over the existing buildings, south across London. The architectural idea used an escalator to take visitors from the ground floor up to a level where the view was framed by a new window in a restaurant. This drawing encapsulates the thinking that developed into the final architectural idea for the new gallery.

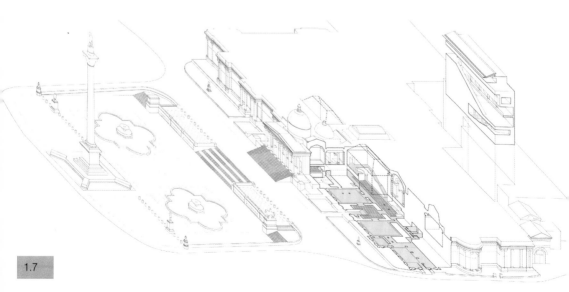

1.7

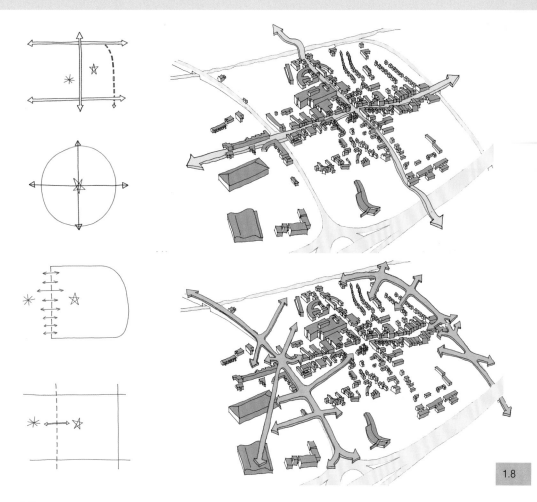

1.8

Project: St Faiths Urban Strategy
Location: Conceptual
Designer: Niall Bird

These diagrammatic sketches analyze aspects of site. This series of drawings pulls together this information as a series of easy-to-read diagrams, which summarize information on roads, boundaries, key buildings and visual connections. To create this kind of analysis, an understanding of the historical evolution of the site is needed.

1 : APPROACH ALONG THE GALATA BRIDGE

2 : CROSSING RIHTIM SQUARE

5 : ENTERING ISTANBUL MODERN

6 : NUSRETIYE CAMII FROM THE ART MODERN

Observational sketches

Observational drawing is an important part of the design process. Careful observation allows us to first absorb and then comprehend what we see. To represent this in a drawing is a learned skill.

To produce an observational drawing first requires an initial period of concentration and analysis. It is important to take the time to really "see". Look carefully at the subject; if it is a street scene or building, look at it in terms of its underlying structure or layout as this will help allow a "plan" to be established for the drawing. Before you put pen to paper consider how your drawing sits on the page and what techniques you will use to render or color the image. The composition of the observational image on the page is key.

1.9a–1.9b

Project: Urban Acupuncture
Location: Istanbul, Turkey
Designer: Adam Parsons

This conceptual proposal is for a series of new buildings in Istanbul, Turkey. The sketches explain how you would approach the scheme as a series of frames. Line weights have been carefully considered to highlight key aspects of the proposal and frame the view. The proposed design has been highlighted in color.

3 : PASSING THE TRAFFIC ON MALIYE ROAD

4 : TRAVELLING ALONG KEMERALTI ROAD

7 : PROMENADE BETWEEN PORT AND WAREHOUSES

8 : MIMAR SINAN UNIVERSITY

1.9a

Framing the sketch

To construct a good observational sketch, visualize the entire view and frame your subject so that it becomes a separate image. Deciding what is important about your sketch, for example, determining those elements of the view that will form the focus of your drawing, is crucial.

Use guidelines to establish your framework. These guides may be a horizontal or vertical axis or other form of reference line on the page. Squares, circles, or other geometric figures can also be used as guides and will help regularize your sketch. By gradually laying these guides on the paper you will be able to organize and place your view and, in doing so, help your drawing develop.

When the framework for the sketch has been established, it serves as an outline for the view. Take the time to check that this outline is correct. It may need to be adjusted to get the proportion and distances right.

Once the framework is correctly established, more line layers can be incorporated to develop detail in the drawing. At each point of addition, the accuracy needs to be checked in order to ensure that the observational integrity of the drawing remains intact. Once all the lines are in place, tone, texture, and color can all be added to the sketch. It is important to "build" drawings in this way so that each stage is clear, and if there are difficulties with proportion, scale, or detail the image can be modified accordingly, again to keep the representation "true".

1.9b

Sketchbooks

Sketchbooks are containers of design information and can take many forms in order to suit different ways of thinking.

Design diaries

A design diary is a sketchbook that is updated daily with thoughts, references, and ideas. It is important that it is treated like a diary—personal, honest, and complete. Some ideas in a design diary will be quickly recorded and never referred to again, while others will have more value and be reworked, developed, and enhanced.

By virtue of its design, a design diary collects ideas and drawings chronologically. Doing so allows concepts to be referenced over time and provides a record of how a project develops and evolves. At certain points, it may be necessary to pause, reflect, and reconsider the design direction. A design diary allows the process of the project to be traced back as a lineage of design development.

1.10a

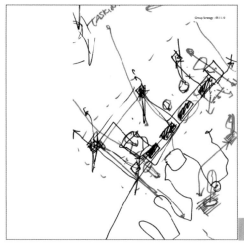

1.10c

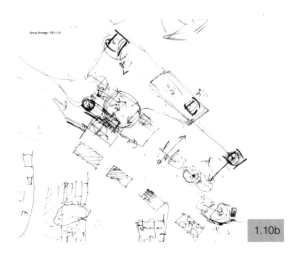

1.10b

1.10d

1.10a–1.10d

Project: Research sketchbook
Location: Conceptual design
Designer: Nick Surtees

These pages from a research journal show areas of investigation for a design project.They are chronological and document the stages of design from observational city sketch, initial exploratory drawings in charcoal, design diagrams, and models. Each sheet has been created digitally.

Research sketchbooks

A research sketchbook is a collection
of ideas and references surrounding a
particular aspect of the design concept;
it may be about a material proposed for
a design idea. In the research sketchbook
the element can be investigated, developed
and shaped into its final form. The research
may be recorded as notes, photographs,
photocopies, or Web images, as well
as sketches.

A research sketchbook will usually contain
the results of investigation outside the
scope of the project. This means that
research sketchbooks are a useful resource
and can suggest new ideas for application
in other contexts. For example, a particular
building material or process that is
thought to be relevant in one scheme may
ultimately prove to be unsuitable. However,
it could contribute to a future project or
idea. This means that all investigations in
research sketchbooks are valid, and so it
is crucial to record and archive them. This
research may be useful in future projects
as well as the current idea.

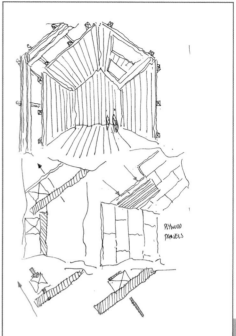

1.11

1.11

Project: Design sketches,
Bursledon Brickworks
Location: Southampton, UK
Designer: Niall Bird

These sketches explore
how new insertions can be
expressed within an existing
building. They work as a
sequence with each linking to
one another. Although different
in scale, they interrogate
form, expression, detail, and
materiality. The inclusion
of scaled figures allows an
understanding of the relative
scale of the proposal.

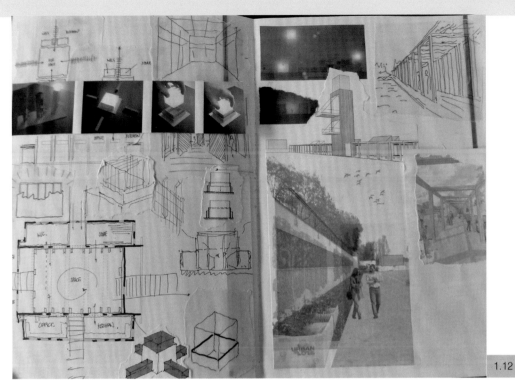

1.12

1.12

Project: Design Diary
Location: Conceptual
Designer: Niall Bird

This page from a student design diary has composite images created from overlaid sketches, model, and drawings of the design proposal. The images also contain research references. The different photographs and sketches explain the thinking behind the architectural idea. The collage has created an overview of the idea's development.

Travel sketchbooks

Travel sketchbooks are specific to a particular journey or experience. They can be used to represent a range of observations about a place or culture. Architects who keep travel sketchbooks may use them to refer back to specific architectural ideas encountered on their travels and reconsider them with their own design projects in mind. Such ideas may include a special use of materials, a specific type of structure, or a particular experience of light affecting a room or a space.

Travel sketches tend to be both observational (describing what is seen) and analytical (analyzing through diagram and ideas, and concepts of design). They will also provide ideas that can be used to inform research and precedent study for design.

Experimental techniques

Developing personal preferences, approaches, and styles is an important aspect of sketching. These can be established through experimentation with drawing styles, techniques, materials, or media. If you see a drawing that you like, find out what materials were used to construct it and then adopt, adapt, and experiment to develop your own individual approach.

Mixing media from a range of different sources can be another way to try new ideas. Different areas of art and design, from illustration and animation to graphic design and fine art, use different representational techniques that can be adapted for architectural drawing and presentation.

Experimental sketching

At the initial stages of a design, the idea can move quickly so the drawings need to keep pace with it. At these points it can be useful and appropriate to draw quick, intuitive lines—a spontaneous type of drawing—to get the idea down on paper. Exploratory sketches need to be more considered; these sort of crafted drawings are used to work through a particular problem, or develop a drawn presentation to explain a scheme.

Sketches don't always have to fall neatly into one of the three types: conceptual, analytical or observational. For example, sketching what we see can be juxtaposed with more abstract drawings. This can be achieved using diagrams and annotated drawings that explore an imagined idea. Sketches can also be moved from one drawing environment to another.

A sketch can be scanned into a computer and further developed with CAD software to become a hybrid drawing that is both freehand and computer generated. Moving between different drawing platforms creates diversity in the sketch and personalizes it even more.

1.13a–13d

Project: Experimental sketch
Location: Conceptual
Designer: Nathan Fairbrother

This series of investigations explores a number of key words, which have been represented as experimental sketches. By recreating the same idea in different mediums such as ink, charcoal or collage, the space between the images can be tested. This space is carefully created through the sketches' composition and the use of collage.

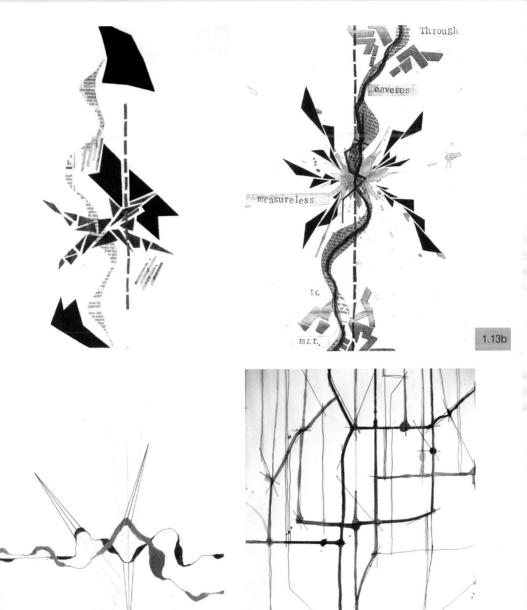

1.13a

1.13b

1.13c

1.13d

Materials and media

Using a black pen on white paper is the traditional sketching approach that architects take, but experimenting with chalk or a white pen on black paper creates an interesting reverse contrast.

Using a different type and width of pencil lead will also change the dynamic of the drawing; a thick piece of graphite can strike bold lines across pieces of paper, whereas a thinner 0.3 mm pencil lead will create more refined and controlled lines.

Using watercolors or colored pencils when sketching can highlight various aspects of the drawing. Watercolors have an added advantage as they can be layered. The first layer can be transparent to give a wash across the page, and subsequent layers of color can be added to provide more depth to the image.

Other techniques

Collage lends an image real texture. A collage image may start as a series of disjointed pieces, which are then carefully organized and placed to create a new composite view of a design idea. The choice of materials for a collage image is important: they may complement one another or be selected to create a deliberate contrast.

In the context of architectural representational techniques, photomontage combines an existing site photograph with a sketch of an architectural idea or proposal, creating a composite image that offers a realistic impression of future architecture. In this sort of image, other elements can be added to lend it a sense of scale. In particular, adding figures and vehicles can provide a sense of scale that is universally recognized, and can also imply the types of activities and events that are associated with the architectural idea.

Concept
Maashaven
Urbanism, European Cities
Unit 403
2006-2007
Jeremy Davies

1.14

**Project: Student housing
proposal
Location: Rotterdam,
The Netherlands
Designer: Jeremy Davies**

This is an external perspective
of a proposal for a student
housing scheme in Rotterdam.
The perspective uses a collage
technique to create an effect
of the skyline and city beyond.
Figures have been included to
give the image a sense of scale
and reality.

Case study: Green House, Australia by Sean Godsell Architects

The Green House is a heritage timber cottage located in inner-suburban Melbourne, Australia. This small, listed building required some additions and alterations. The client wanted a new house, but the existing cottage on the site was considered historically significant. As a result, the front section of the cottage needed to be retained with a discrete new building constructed at the rear.

The architects used freehand drawings at a range of scales to describe the process of design. The drawings included perspective sketches of the interior, CAD modeling and a set of detail drawings of the construction information. The freehand nature of the drawings gives a distinctive and individualistic visual description of the design ideas. The drawings evolved during the design process to suit the client's needs.

During the construction drawing process, detail drawings were also made for the building contractor, who required a different set of drawings that suited his requirements. These drawings explore material connections and details at scales from full size or 1:1 or interior scale (see page 37).

The project was inspired by Japanese architects such as Kazuo Shinohara and his House in White and House in Hanayama No 3, and Tadao Ando's Row House in Sumiyoshi. These houses use very simple architectural ideas, which explore the interior space of the building; freehand drawing is an effective way to draw these spaces.

The cottage interior was remodeled to have a cathedral type of ceiling in terms of its height, with a pair of timber posts supporting the ridge beam and two light cannons directing light to the center of the single space formed by the demolition of an existing wall. These ideas were explored through many perspective sketches to give an impression of the possibilities of the interior space.

A small courtyard bound by concrete walls separates the cottage from the small addition, evoking the "Row House" in the process. The roof of the addition was constructed in glass, with an automated timber sunscreen. The sunscreen protects the occupant from summer sun, but it can be configured in a variety of ways to allow the winter sun to enter. As the screens are moved, the appearance of the building changes.

Although this is a small and modest house design, it has a powerful concept, and it creates simple but impressive spaces filled with light. The freehand sketches communicate the impressive nature of the interior spaces.

1.15a

1.15b

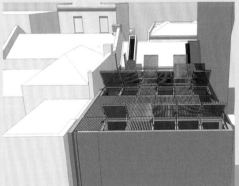

1.15c

1.15a–1.15c

Project: Green House
Location: Melbourne, Australia
Architect: Sean Godsell

These pen drawings work as a sequence and include detail sketches that interrogate the detail of the roof design (1.15a) and interior views (1.15b). The sketches explore how materials might come together to ensure that the roof panels can be configured in numerous ways.

The perspective sketch is constructed around the structural frame and focuses on the columns and beams. The inclusion of a person and representation of materiality on the roof and floor gives a sense of depth.

The CAD model (1.15c) shows the detail of the roof in an open position. The materials of the roof panels are illustrated as timber and the proposal grey. The model illustrates the adjoining buildings, which create the central courtyard

Project: City sketchbook

Designers learn by seeing the world, and exploring and describing what is immediately in front of them. Keeping a city sketchbook of visual observations is a good discipline, which will improve understanding of spaces and places.

Many of the world's architects and designers have enjoyed recording their travels and exploring the cities of the world. With a sketchbook as a companion, travel gives us time to reflect and learn from the experiences around us.

Observing and sketching what we experience imprints an understanding on our minds. It allows us to identify what we wish to emphasize. Unlike a photograph, which aims to capture the image, we as the observer select what to record and draw.

City drawing kit

The materials and equipment needed for city sketching must be simple and practical as they need to be carried and easily accessible:

- Small hardback sketchbook to ensure a firm surface
- Variety of pens and pencils
- Graphite stick or charcoal
- Drawing ink and sketching pen
- A selection of colored pencils.

Process

This exercise is about observation, freehand drawing, and practice. If you make a mistake, do not rub it out and start again. Draw lightly, or in pencil, first and then make the line more definite when you are more confident. This step-by-step guide will teach you how to observe the city and draw what you see by testing a variety of techniques. To create a skyline drawing you will need a sketchbook, pencil, and sketching pen.

1 Observe the city skyline and identify key markers that give the view structure. For example, buildings on the horizon such as churches or tower blocks.

2 Divide the sheet with horizontal and vertical guidelines in pencil or fine sketching pen. This will act as your drawing grid (1.16b).

3 Use the grid to draw a continuous line mapping the horizon and key features within the skyline. Observe the edges of buildings, roof forms, and heights in relation to the grid (1.16c).

4 Observe the details of the building form and infill the framework with the details of the facades. Add perspective to give depth to the sketch (1.16d).

5 Use overlaid drawings or thicker pen weights to emphasize the key features— for example, the horizon or buildings in the foreground (1.16a).

6 Annotate your drawings to explain thoughts and observations. Color can be used to draw focus to key features.

1.16a

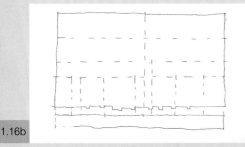

1.16b

1.16c

1.16d

Explore observational drawing

Redraw the view of the city and test the following techniques:

1 Draw the skyline in one continuous line while leaving the pen/pencil on the page.

2 Divide you page into four and create a series of observational drawings as you move through a public place within the city.

3 Redraw one of your observational sketches using shadow only.

4 Create a series of analytical sketches that use a plan or section to help to understand the city.

5 Use a variety of media and colors to draw textures in response to the city.

1.16a–1.16d

Project: City sketch
Location: New York, USA
Architect: Lorraine Farrelly

These four sketches are part of a sequence that describes how to construct a city view.

2.1

2 Scale

Scale has multiple meanings in architecture. Drawings can be to scale (adhering to an established or agreed reference or system), "out of", or "not to" scale. Historically, architects have employed a range of scale systems. Classical Greek and Roman architecture, for example, used a modular system of measurement. In classical architecture, each module was the width of the column base, and this was used to determine the classical system of orders and their relative proportioning. Le Corbusier also used a modular system based on the proportions of the human body, which ensured that his architectural designs related to human scale.

To represent a space or building, comparative scale systems are needed to design, develop, and explain the architectural idea. Plan, section, and elevation drawings and models are the conventions used to communicate the idea; however, they need to be created using a system that can be measured and understood by the architect, builder, and client alike.

When drawing to scale, the right scale system needs to be used for the appropriate context. Smaller- or larger-scale investigations will lend themselves better to different types of projects. For example, the design of a city will be better understood in large scale, whereas the design of a piece of furniture will necessitate a smaller-scale system and drawing.

Understanding scale is to connect with the relative size of cities, places, buildings, spaces, and objects and to learn how they in turn connect with one another and the people that occupy and use them.

2.1

Project: Phare Tower
Location: Paris, France
Architect: Morphosis
Architects

This schematic design by Morphosis is a proposal for a structure in the Parisian district of La Défense; the Phare Tower is a 300-meter-high commercial building. This computer-generated photomontage provides an idea of the impressive scale of the proposed structure.

Measuring

Buildings can be quantitatively described by measuring them in different ways, for example, by quantifying the amounts of materials required to build them, or by understanding the size of their internal and external spaces.

Measuring existing buildings is important when there is an intention to extend, renovate, or redevelop a structure, as it allows the architect to suggest how best to respond to various openings in walls, floors, and roofs. There is also much to be learned from studying and measuring an existing building; doing so can provide an understanding of how it has been put together, what materials have been used, or particular details of its construction. To take a building and explore it via the plan, section, and elevation details will explain many aspects of the original design concept.

Measurement systems

Measuring systems are universally agreed or understood. Today, we commonly use metric or imperial systems of measurement. The metric system uses millimeters (mm), centimeters (cm), meters (m), and kilometers (km) as its basic units of measurement, and the imperial system uses units of inches (in), feet (ft), yards (yd), and miles (mi).

In addition to these standard conventions, modular systems use an understood "module" as their basic unit of measurement. For example, in classical architecture the understood module was the width of the base of the column. Le Corbusier's *Le Modulor* (1948) divided the body into units and his architectural drawings related to this system of measurement (see page 35).

2.2

Project: Design proposal for
Bursledon Brickworks
Location: Southampton, UK
Designer: Robert Cox

These drawings examine the details of a building using section, elevation, and detail drawings. There is sufficient detail to understand the size and dimensions of the materials used in both the interior and exterior of the building.

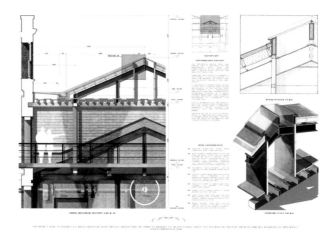

Survey

To better understand how measurements in architecture work, buildings and spaces that already exist can be measured and drawn. When an existing space is measured and reproduced as a drawing it is referred to as a "survey".

A site survey will consist of plans that explain the site's boundaries, section drawings that will describe the site's landscape and important surrounding features. The different site levels will be indicated as map contours or as a series of spot heights that show relative height.

Information about the site and its boundaries can be mapped digitally from a number of online providers. For a fee, any site plan available on the database can be downloaded, printed, and used as a basis for a CAD drawing (subject to certain copyright rules). These websites have facilitated an easier connection of a design idea with a site.

Measured dimensioned drawings

It is usual to apply numerical dimensions to measured drawings as this allows the information to be read accurately and easily. These dimensions may be displayed as a series of individual measurements or as a running dimension.

When undertaking a survey, it is important to measure the spaces individually and then incorporate running dimensions that measure the overall space or building— these act as check measurements.

Drawing scale ratio

Architects and spatial designers tend to have a range of scales that respond to the design of the various spaces that they are engaged with. The scales are defined as a ratio regardless of whether the measurement system is imperial or metric scale.

Metric scale	Imperial scale	Drawing use
1:1	Full size	Details
1:2	Half size	Details
1:5	3" = 1'-0"	Details
1:10	1 1/2" = 1'-0"	Interior spaces/furniture
1:20	3/4" = 1'-0"	Interior spaces/furniture
1:50	1/4" = 1'-0"	Interior spaces/furniture/detailed
	(equivalent 1" = 4.17')	floor plans
1:100	1/8" = 1'-0"	Building plans/layouts
	(equivalent 1" = 8.33')	
1:200	1/16" = 1'–0"	
	(equivalent 1" = 16.66')	
1:500	1" = 40'-0"	Building plans/site plans
1:1000	1" = 80'-0"	Urban scale for site/locations plans
1:1250	1" = 100'	Site plans
1:2500	1" = 250'	Site plans/city maps
NTS		Not to scale (abstract)

Sizes are closest approximation

Equipment

In order to obtain and record precise measurements in a scale drawing, calibrated equipment is needed. The most basic scale-drawing tool is a scale rule, which is specifically dimensioned to give precise measurements.

Different sorts of designers will use different sorts of scale rules. For example, an engineer and a product designer will use different scale systems as references in their design work and so will need to use different types of scale rule that work within these systems to record the measurements.

When surveying spaces, a tape measure is a basic, but essential, piece of equipment. Tape measures are available in a variety of sizes and again the most suitable size will depend on the scale of the object or space to be measured. For example, a three-meter tape measure is useful for small-dimensioned spaces and objects, but if measuring a building it will be useless, and a 30-meter tape (approximately 100 ft) will suit this purpose far better. In addition to traditional tape measures, digital devices will accurately measure a room or building using laser-beam technology.

To understand the different levels across a site, a theodolite is necessary. A theodolite is an instrument with a rolling telescope that is used for measuring both horizontal and vertical angles. It will be placed at a particular point on a site to create an ordnance datum for the site; from that point all levels can be described relative to that datum. A large site can have a considerable range of levels, and this can affect the subsequent design or scheme layout.

2.3a–2.3b

Project: Lawn House
Location: Lusatian, Germany
Architect: CJ Lim/Studio 8 Architects

These drawings were created as part of a competition to propose a new type of housing. The proposal is for a series of floating green lawns that emphasize the tranquillity of the lake. The lawns are also tennis courts—on the plan you can see the white-line markings. The 3D visualization shows the wider context of the lake.

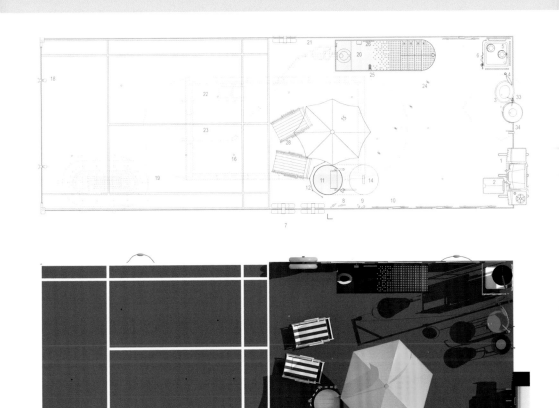

2.3a

2.3b

Full size

A building proposal can sometimes benefit from full-size exploration. Renaissance architects favored this technique and often made full-size representations of elements of proposed buildings (such as their dome or cupola structure) to give an impression of a new building form.

In cases of specialized construction, it may be that a component needs to be made at full size to ensure that it will fit its intended context. Or there may be a need for experimentation; a particular element of the architectural scheme may need to be tested as a full-size piece (in the same way that a prototype may be constructed in product design or engineering) to ensure that it works properly. There may also be innovative aspects of the design scheme that need to be built at full size in order to be properly understood.

Full-size staging, drawing and modeling

Some spaces can be "staged" to suggest a building or object in context. The use of disposable materials, such as cardboard or polystyrene, can create an impression of the intended design at full size and so allow a better understanding of its impact within a space. Such pieces can also be read as installations: as full-size pieces of sculpture in a space.

Generally, drawing or modeling at full size will be restricted to architectural details (such as a door handle or a piece of furniture), for example, where the type, texture, and tactility of the materials used are important design considerations. There may also be specific fixing details that need to be developed from particular components, and made full size and tested as a prototype.

Virtually full size

For most architecture, it is only at the point when the concept is finally constructed that there can be a real understanding of the full-scale impact of the building's form, materiality, and scale. However, advances in technology now mean that it's possible for a proposed form to be virtually tested in its surroundings.

This technology has been developed in tandem with the computer gaming industry, and it allows the architect to develop their virtual spaces, rooms, cities, and environments and suggest how we (or the user) may interact with their ideas.

By using specialized equipment, one can virtually experience a proposed space at full size. This can be an impressive experience, transporting you to a world where you can open virtual doors and move through imagined spaces. The boundaries between architectural vision and reality are now being challenged.

These watercolor drawings are a full-size representation of a door handle. Drawing something full size allows it to be understood in terms of material and scale.

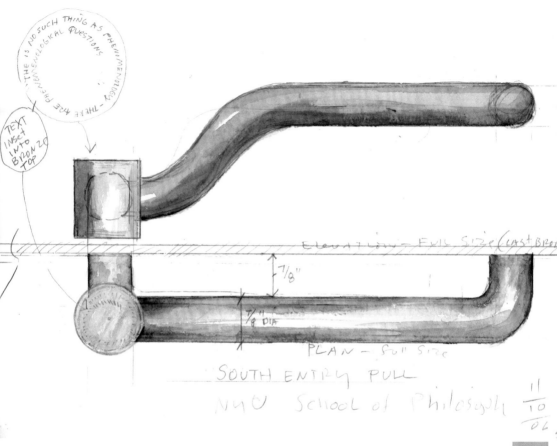

Within the drawing (handwritten annotations):
THE IS NO SUCH THING AS PHENOMENOLOGICAL QUESTIONS – THERE ARE PHENOMENOLOGICAL...

TEXT INSET INTO BRONZE TOP

ELEVATION – FULL SIZE (CAST BRON...

7/8"

7/8" DIA

PLAN – FULL SIZE

SOUTH ENTRY PULL

NYU School of Philosophy 11/10/06 s

2.4

2.4
_____

Project: Door handle
Location: School of
Philosophy, New York, USA
Architect: Steven Holl
Architects

This is a full-size watercolor
drawing of a door handle
intended for the School of
Philosophy in New York.
Drawing something full size
allows it to be understood in
terms of material and scale. It is
beautifully drawn in pencil with
accents of color.

2.5

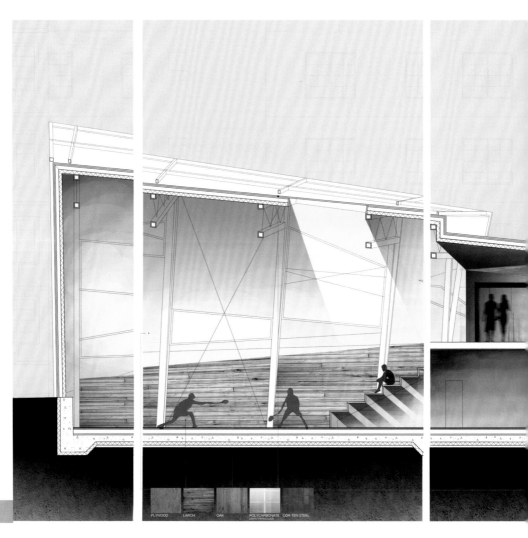

PLYWOOD   LARCH   OAK   POLYCARBONATE   COR-TEN STEEL
                          LEXAN THERMOCLEAR

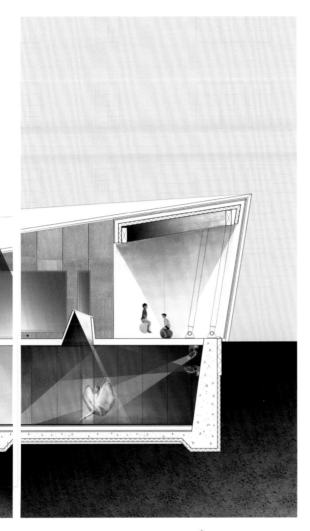

2.5

**Project: Sports complex
Location: Brighton, UK
Designer: Aivita Mateika**

This section drawing shows the relationship between interior spaces and the activities within them. The long section has been cut to express the different volumes and how they are connected. The drawing is a staggered section cut to express how the roof form changes as you move through the building. The inclusion of scaled people, materials, and light give depth to the interior.

Detail scale

Detailed scale drawings allow an in-depth investigation of a building or space through close inspection of its proposed component parts. Detail drawings will form part of the full set of information about the proposed architecture and will relate to other drawings and information in the scheme design. These drawings are usually composed at scales of 1:2 half full size, 1:5 a fifth full size, or 1:10 a tenth full size (see page 37). This full set of drawings then describes a building from site and location through to material detail and finish.

In any given building, some details are generic and will apply throughout using standard building and construction techniques and materials, but there will also be more specialized details; these need to be designed and developed to respond to particular, and perhaps unique, conditions of the building.

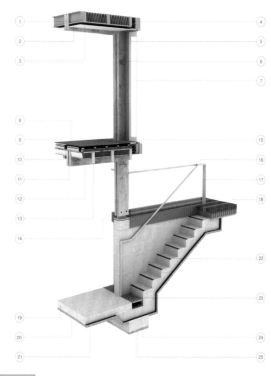

2.6

2.6

Project: Bursledon Brickworks
Location: Southampton, UK
Designer: David Holden

This detailed section drawing cuts through a timber insertion designed to fit within an existing building. It is drawn in perspective, so it has a sense of depth and considers how elements of the building come together. The numbered labels describe the proposed materials (not shown here).

Detail drawings

When creating a package of detail drawings, each detail needs to be considered in relationship to the whole building; the concept of the whole scheme should be visible in each of the detail drawings. It is, for example, the touch of a door handle or the relationship between a wall and a floor that, when the building is inhabited, has the most impact on our personal experience of the architecture. The approach to designing these sorts of details needs to have the same rigor as the design of the building's plan and section. The detail drawings represent the subtlety of the architectural idea and provide an understanding of how materials can come together in a way that is sympathetic to the concept.

When a building is being constructed on-site, the detail drawings can be modified as the construction progresses (if need be) to respond to issues on-site, varying material availability, or changes in the design. Detail drawings usually contain clear written information. This text is usually supplied as an accompanying key, legend, or numbered reference that explains the materials.

Assembly drawings

Assembly drawings are mechanical and engineering forms of representation that explore the "assembly" of different component parts. These drawings are often standard instructions that suggest a uniform approach to putting materials together. This approach will be informed by manufacturer's information and guidelines about their products. In many cases, these details are further developed by the architect to suit the specific conditions of a building.

Details of a building's assembly and construction need to be explored at a range of scales. For example, the scale of understanding needs to allow expression of fixings such as nuts, bolts, and screws. To describe this clearly, drawing scales of 1:2 and 1:5 need to be employed (see page 37).

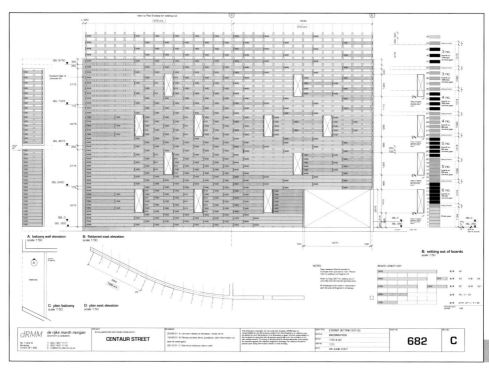

2.7a–2.7c

Project: Centaur Street Housing
Location: London, UK
Architect: dRMM

Image 2.7a sets out the building's curved elevation. It enabled the designer to create a detailed study of the cladding of the complex curved façade, and it was also used to help explain how they intended the building to be built.

The assembly detail drawings (2.7b and 2.7c) show the key details at 1:5 scale. All of the plans are cross-referenced to the 1:20 sections.

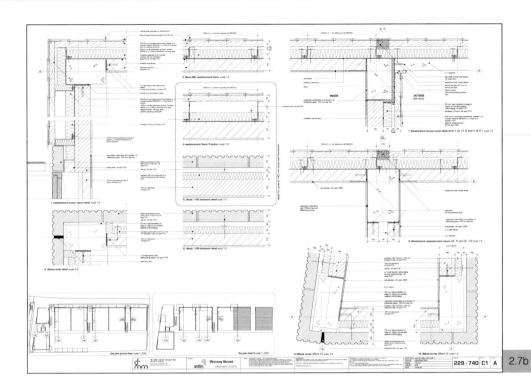

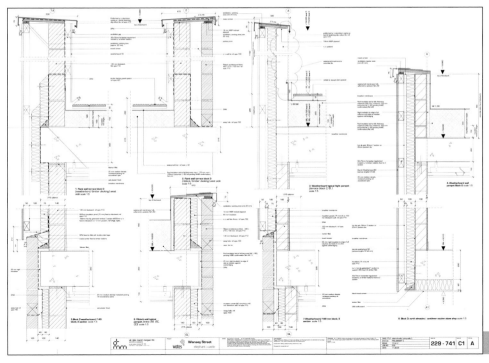

2.8

Project: The Eco-Station
Location: Various sites in
the UK
Designers: David Yearley,
Lorraine Farrelly, Matt
Mardell, Alex Wood and
Architecture PLB

The Eco-Station was a structure
meant to engage the public with
the concept of sustainability.
It was designed as a series
of frames that could easily be
assembled and taken apart at
a range of locations. It was then
clad with panels using materials
from recycled mobile phones to
old plastic pipes.

Detail section drawings

A section drawing will display the internal
structure of a building (or space) as if it has
been cut through vertically or horizontally.
A detailed section drawing can show the
relationship between the critical details
within the sectional planes. A section
through an external wall, for example, can
describe its relationship with the building's
foundation, its floors, and its roof.

These drawings are most often produced
at scales of 1:10 or 1:20 (see page 37)
depending on the size of the building. Detail
section drawings are cross-referenced to
the relevant section drawing so that the
context of the detail can be understood in
relation to the rest of the building.

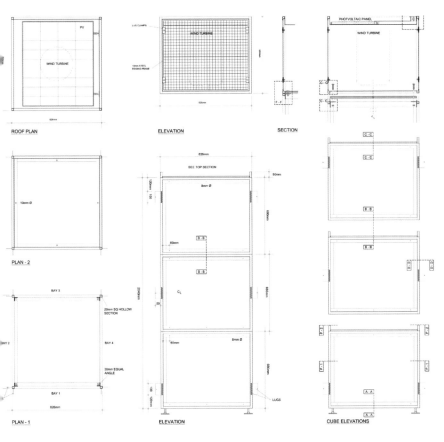

ROOF PLAN   ELEVATION   SECTION

PLAN - 2

PLAN - 1   ELEVATION   CUBE ELEVATIONS

2.8

Specialized drawing packages

Details are drawn to describe their particular conditions, functions, or context within a scheme. Certain elements of a scheme (such as a staircase or piece of furniture) may have to be built by manufacturers that are not closely associated with the project. In such cases, a package of bespoke or specialized drawings is compiled. These drawings will contain sufficient information to allow the details to be produced separately and correctly.

Isolating the manufacture of building components in this way allows the scheme design to develop more flexibly and to be informed by a range of different specialists.

Interior scale

When drawing interior spaces, an important consideration is that the whole space needs to be described at once. Doing so allows an understanding between the furniture in the space, the detailed components of the space (such as its light fittings), and the material finish of the space.

Interior space is normally described at 1:10 and 1:20 scale (see page 37), depending on the size of the room. These drawings are even more effective if they display objects where we understand the scale.

For example, if we see a scale drawing of a room with a bed in it, then we can better understand the scale of the room relative to the furniture. This is because a bed is a (largely) uniformly sized object. A scale drawing of a room with a table in it will be less effective as a table can vary in size.

Placing figures of people in interior drawings also allows the viewer to connect with the scale of the room or the space, and develop an idea of how the space might be utilized.

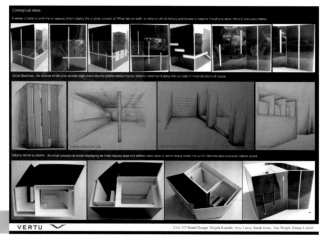

2.9

2.9

Project: Vertu retail store
Location: Conceptual
Architect: Group Design

This series of images describes the development of interior design ideas for a mobile phone store. The concept started with a series of models that were photographed from inside to explore the spaces created. Interior sketches then explored the intended views within the store.

Sample panels

When designing an interior space, the use of color, texture, available light, and finish are also key considerations that contribute to an overall scheme. These aspects of design can be varied to produce an array of interior experiences. Much like perspective drawings (see page 120), sample panels or material boards can suggest how the finish of the interior could be executed.

Sample panels can show color schemes and the finishes of wall coverings and flooring materials; they can also specify particular interior details such as door handles or timber finishes, which may be included to give a real-size example of the intended finish.

BAY ELEVATION 1 - 1 SCALE 1:50

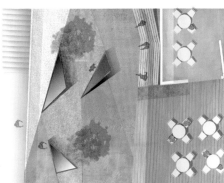

MATERIALS

CONCRETE

CORTEN

LARCH SHADERS

GLAZING

COMPOSITE
WOOD DECKING

PEBBLES

BLACK BASALT SAWN
PAVING

HISTORIC WALL

2.10

2.10
_____

Project: Conceptual project
Location: Brighton, UK
Designer: Aivita Mateika

This section and bay elevation is drawn through both interior and exterior spaces and is linked to a materials board. It gives a view into the public space between the buildings. The inclusion of photorealistic materials gives a suggestion of the final scheme.

Interior and sectional perspective

Interior perspective drawings are a useful way to describe the intended function of a room or space. At interior scale, the sense of interaction that the potential user might have with the space, its atmosphere, or how they may use it can be communicated.

Often, an interior perspective drawing is combined with a section drawing so that the activity that might take place inside the room is conjoined with the sense of how the building is constructed and what the relationships between the interior spaces are. These sectional perspectives connect the viewer with the space more directly by associating the building with a potential experience.

2.11

Project: Student housing scheme
Location: Rotterdam, The Netherlands
Designer: Jeremy Davies

This proposed housing project used an innovative idea for student accommodation. It comprises a series of large-scale "trunks" that are self-contained storage, sleeping, and study areas. The detail drawing and interior perspective give a good idea of the scale of the design and show how students can inhabit the "rooms". The proposal is a unique solution to a common interior spaces challenge.

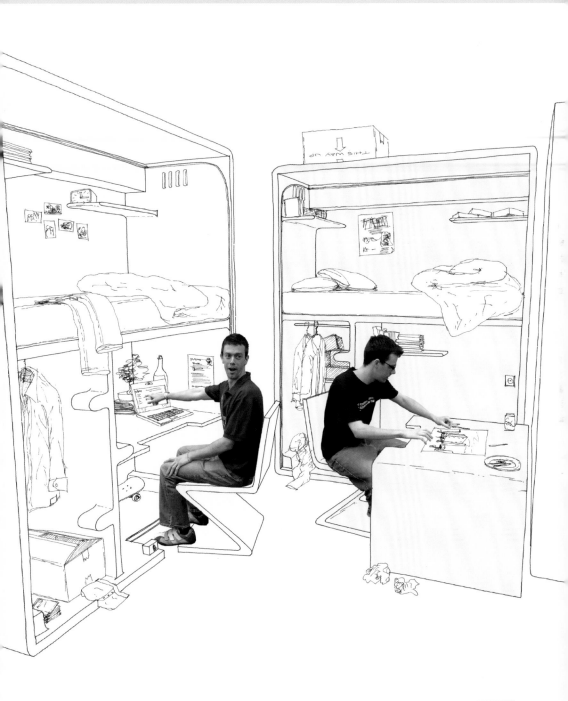

2.11

Building scale

Describing a building accurately will incorporate a variety of scales, but selecting the appropriate scale will depend on the size of the building design.

A small house can be drawn at 1:50 scale which will show (in relative detail) the building and its suggested furniture layout. A larger house or building, however, would be insufficiently described at 1:50 scale and would need to be described at a minimum of 1:100 scale. A larger development, perhaps a development for a block of apartments, would need to be described at a minimum of 1:200 scale. If aspects of landscape and the external surrounding area are important, 1:500 may be used (but this scale is relatively diagrammatic). (See page 37.)

2.12

Project: Bursledon Brickworks
Location: Southampton, UK
Architect: Robert Cox

This long-section drawing of Bursledon Brickworks describes the relationship between the various rooms within the building and sets it into a wider context. The section gives a glimpse into the interior in a way we could not experience in reality. The inclusion of people allows us to read scale and shows how the rooms interlink.

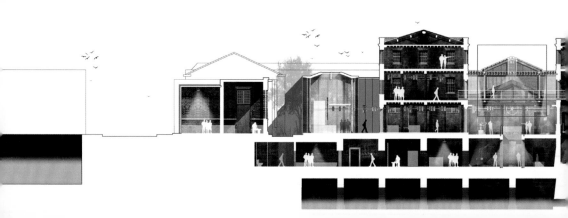

Building drawings

A set of building drawings should contain enough information so that one can understand all the spatial connections within the scheme as well as the details of its internal layout. It is important to show intended furniture layout in the design as this will help the viewer gain a better understanding of the use of the space. The drawings need to collectively describe the whole building as a series of rooms, along with their associated functions.

These building drawings will be further separated into groups to allow different types of information to be described and further developed. For example, a reflected ceiling plan will describe the layout of the lights and other electrical fittings and their location on the building's ceiling. Other layouts might describe furniture configurations, the building's electrical wiring, or its heating and ventilation systems. Each piece of information will be described on a different drawing in order to allow clarity and accuracy when designing each of the building's component systems.

Shifting scales

When designing a building, the process normally begins with a consideration of site and location, then progresses to the proposal's immediate context. Next, the building layout needs to be developed to ensure that it connects with aspects of route, views, and orientation. Finally, detailed consideration is given to the building's materials, components, and assembly.

At each stage of design, the drawing scale shifts. Location drawings are created at a scale of 1:1250 (see page 37). The next stage of drawings will show more detail, describing form and relationship to site; these drawings will be created at 1:500 scale. Building layout drawings are produced at 1:200 and 1:100 scale to allow the relationships between rooms, spaces, functions, and connections to outside spaces to be understood.

All of these drawings can be developed simultaneously and, in some cases, this is preferable because certain drawings (such as plans and sections) need to constantly relate to one another as the building's design is developed, updated, and realized.

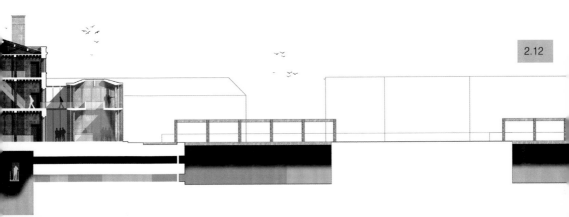

2.12

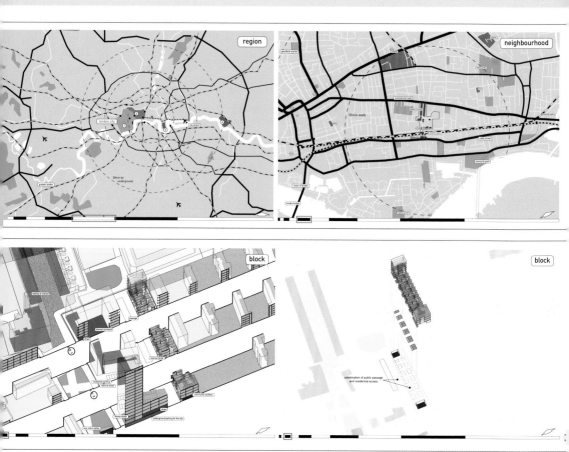

2.13

**Project: Darling
Redevelopment
Location: London, UK
Architect: S333**

This series of drawings helps
explain the range of scales that
are needed to communicate
an architectural idea. The first
drawing is a map created
at an urban scale and then
each successive drawing
incorporates more detail about
the architectural scheme,
providing information about
the surrounding region, the
neighborhood, the development
site, the apartment block, and,
finally, the apartment interior.

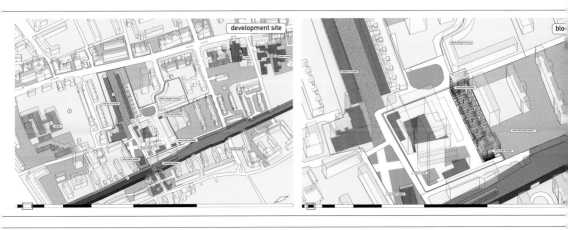

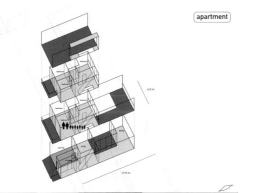

2.13

"A great building must begin with the unmeasurable, must go through measurable means when it is being designed and in the end must be unmeasurable."
Louis Kahn

Urban scale

Cities contain a variety of buildings and spaces (such as parks, schools, shops, apartments, or hospitals) that are all united by a network of infrastructures or routes (for example, roads and railway lines). Understanding how all these buildings (or spaces) and routes connect with one another requires the use of scale that cartographers and town planners use: urban (or map) scale. Maps of districts and cities are commonly described using scales of 1:10000, 1:5000, and 1:2500 (see page 37). When drawing at urban scale, deciding what to include and what to omit is of primary importance. A map is a constructed image and as such should only describe what is necessary within its particular frame of reference.

Using an urban scale in architectural drawing allows a deeper analysis of the site because its location can be described in terms of its relationships with other aspects of the city. Many architectural developments in cities form part of an urban strategy; this is a connected design concept that unfolds across a city linking different spaces, buildings, and districts.

Some buildings are designed at a vast scale, incorporating parks or promenades, or even suggesting new ways of living in the city. To describe these ideas and concepts, a whole section of a city or area needs to be drawn at a map scale of 1:1000 or 1:2500.

Google Earth

In 1977, Charles and Ray Eames investigated the concept of scale and presented their results in *Powers of Ten*. This nine-minute film was an investigation into the relative scale of objects and spaces. Starting from a view of two people enjoying a picnic, the film transports the viewer to the outer edges of the known universe. Every ten seconds, the picnic spot starting point is seen from ten times farther out, until our own galaxy becomes just a speck of light. The return journey moves inwards at ten times more magnification every ten seconds, until the viewer reaches the hand of one of the picnickers. The journey ends inside a proton of a carbon atom within a DNA molecule in a white blood cell.

The Internet now offers a similar facility via Google's Google Earth, Google Earth Pro, and Street View software (www.google.com/earth).

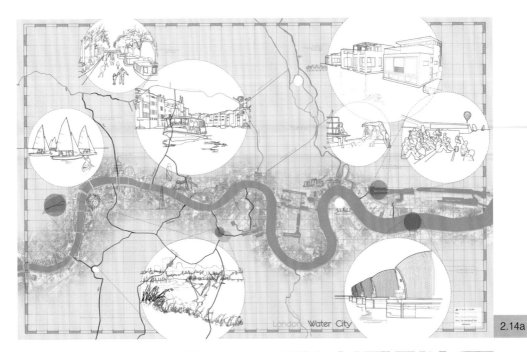

2.14a

2.14a–2.14b

Project: Water City
Location: London, UK
Designer: Sophie Bellows

Image 2.14a shows London as
an abstract map. Drawn at the
scale of the city, you can read
the pattern of rivers through
central London and the streets.
Blue is used to highlight the
importance of water. As an
overall composition, this map
uses grids to provide scale and
is overlaid with a series of serial
views imagining London as if it
were Venice.

The plan shown in image 2.14b
locates the site for a housing
proposal within the water
city strategy. The plan
provides information about
the immediate context by
displaying surrounding
buildings and landscape.

2.14b

Figure and ground mapping

Giambattista Nolli was a seventeenth-century cartographer who described aspects of space in Rome using a technique called "figure and ground mapping". This technique sees buildings displayed as areas of solid blocks and urban spaces are left as clear (or empty) areas. The figure and ground mapping technique is particularly useful when analyzing a site to better understand the density of urban spaces.

Maps and mapping

Mapping is a generic term that is used architecturally to describe the relative location of a place or site. But the term can also be applied to the way in which places might be described. A place may be mapped using diagrams, models or drawings.

The location of a site is the starting point for most architecture. Information such as where the site is, what the site orientation is, or whether or not there are any interesting geographical features nearby can be found in a location map, but moreover, location maps can also suggest important considerations for a design (as the scheme could respond to existing buildings and facilities in the area).

Location maps are usually described at the scale of 1:1250 or 1:1000. A scale of 1:500 (see page 37) may also be used to show details of the site's immediate context and surrounding location, particularly in urban areas.

2.15

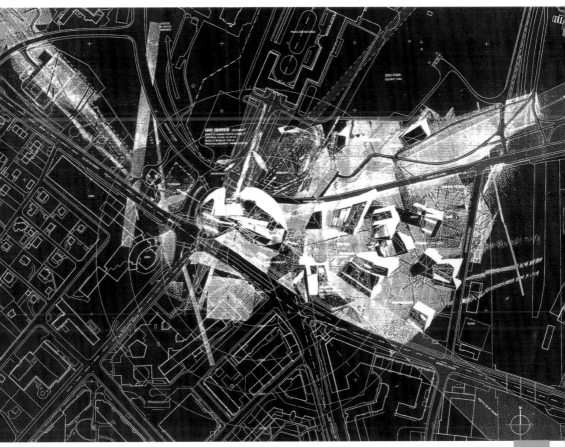

2.16

2.15

Project: Figure ground urban analysis
Location: Chichester, UK
Designer: Khalid Saleh

These maps analyze Chichester's city center. The use of black images on a white background, and the reverse of white images on a black background, create a contrast and allow an easy understanding of the spaces between buildings and density within the city plan.

2.16

Project: Cloud #9
Location: Geneva, Switzerland
Architect: Coop Himmelb(l)au

The idea of the Cloud #9 scheme is to propose architecture that is as buoyant and changeable as the clouds. The white sketch layered over the plan appears fluid and fluctuating against the static plan of the city. The drawing is inverted so appears to be a white line over a black background.

Not to scale

Drawings that are "not to scale" (NTS) are, as the name suggests, created when scale is unnecessary to explain an idea or concept. If a drawing or model is conceptual, then its scale is irrelevant; of primary importance are the form, the idea, and the materials. Scale provides a comparative reference, so producing drawings or models that are NTS allows a different sort of consideration; there is a freedom to investigate the architectural design using other parameters. The most often-used NTS representational techniques are conceptual designs, experimental models, sketches, photomontages, and collages.

Conceptual designs

Particularly appropriate at the initial stages of a project when developing a concept or preliminary design, conceptual drawings allow the architect to move freely through their ideas. The concept can be developed diagrammatically in sketches, or via an investigation of model form, shape, or material.

At the conceptual stage of an architectural scheme, anything can inform the design development; it may be a process of making or thinking, or a physical sense of form or materiality.

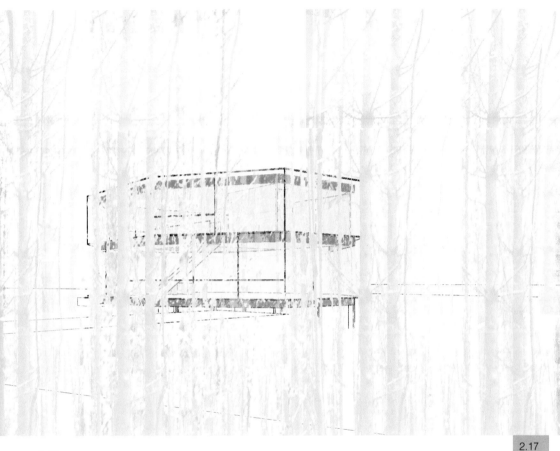

2.17

2.17

Project: Rough Grounds
Location: Gloucestershire, UK
Architect: Pierre d'Avoine
Architects

This is one of a group of houses that forms an integral part of a larger rural development for an equestrian center. This perspective drawing shows the house viewed through a veil of trees. Octagon House, Belvedere House, and the Lodge have been designed together with indoor and outdoor schools and stables embedded in clearings formed within the woodland plantation known as "Rough Grounds".

Experimental modeling

Investigating a proposed architectural design via modeling and sculpting allows the form to be developed through the manipulation of shapes, planes, lines and edges. This design process uses the properties of the modeling material to create architectural form. Scale is not an initial consideration. Experimental modeling is definitely driven by the idea that a building's form follows its function.

Sketching

Most sketches are not created to scale. These drawings are created for observational, analytical, or developmental purposes. This is the advantage of sketching: it allows you to work through a design problem visually and to develop your response to it iteratively. Similarly, diagrams used in site or building analysis are not necessarily drawn to scale; often, these communicate a specific idea or understanding of a building or space and, as such, scale is again irrelevant.

Photomontage and collage

Photomontage and collage work are not created to any particular scale as the intention underlying these forms of representation is the communication of the architectural idea. These artistic investigations and presentations offer the opportunity to visually explore an idea in a dynamic way and suggest both impossible and possible scenarios and situations.

2.18

2.18

Project: Wansey Street social housing
Location: London, UK
Architect: dRMM

The Wansey Street social housing scheme reinterprets the standard British terrace house with twenty-first century requirements for density, planning flexibility, sustainability, ownership, and security. This perspective drawing gives a glimpse into the courtyard space, and it also describes the elevation of the proposed development and how the building connects with the courtyard design.

Case study: The Gherkin, UK by Foster + Partners

Sometimes the range of scales for drawings for a new building can be from one extreme to another. A large project may need drawings that are at a scale of a city, like a map. However, when the building is built on-site, drawings at a much larger scale are needed to describe material connections— for example, where a door or window fits into a building.

The Gherkin—as it is commonly known because of its unique form—is a skyscraper designed by Foster + Partners at 30 St Mary Axe in London. The original client and occupants were Swiss Reinsurance, a global insurance company. The building's aerodynamic shape maximizes the natural lighting and ventilation, and it has a clearly distinctive approach to environmental design. The building uses 50 percent less energy than other similar air-conditioned office buildings. Fresh air is drawn up through the structure to naturally ventilate it. In addition, it maximizes natural daylight with reduced reliance on artificial lighting. All these design decisions influenced the final form of the building.

There are over 5,000 triangular and diamond-shaped panels, and they vary at each level. Each of these panels had to be drawn in detail before they could be manufactured.

Such a distinctive building has a set of drawings that can be read at a range of levels. They needed to present the image of the building in its context as an identifiable landmark. It also needs to be represented as a technical environmental system, with drawings that provide a level of information that allow engineers to develop the systems, and manufacturers and constructors to build it.

For this building, the drawings needed to be both abstract and defined. The plan is circular and also tapered, so at each level a new plan needed to be generated with the core element of the structure and access. The circular plan has an interesting relationship to its building plot, which is rectangular, allowing for a landscaped area around the base of the building.

The building's design was achieved by using specialist CAD software. The form features a set of progressive curves and was both designed and presented using parametric computer-modeling techniques. The shape and geometry have affinities with forms that recur in nature. The external diagonal steel structure is, because of its triangulated geometry, both strong and light, allowing a flexible, column-free interior space.

This scheme illustrates the importance of the CAD drawing, which can facilitate new forms and shapes. Also, the building has a simple form, which belies a very complex system of engineering and material manufacture. The building can be drawn as a simple form against the London skyline as a sketch, but is also represented as a series of complex engineering components for manufacture. It has become iconic because of this form, but simplicity in form often requires some complexity in process, design, thinking, and drawing.

2.19a

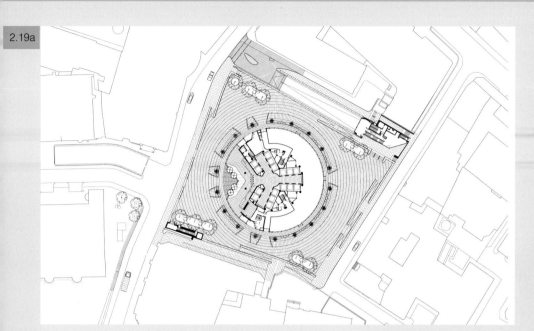

2.19b

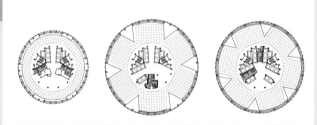

2.19c

2.19a–2.19c

Project: The Gherkin
Location: London, UK
Architect: Foster + Partners

Image 2.19a shows the ground-floor plan presented in the context of the immediate buildings. This allows the landscape proposals to be represented at the base of the building.

Image 2.19b shows a sequence of floor plans taken from various levels throughout the building. The plan is circular and tapered so at each level a new plan needed to be generated to reveal the core elements of the structure and access.

Image 2.19c shows the top floor of the Gherkin and reveals the curved glass paneling forming the top of the building.

Project: Survey

Scale is about proportion, size, and measuring. To understand drawing scale you need to understand the real size of spaces and objects and how this relates to our own physical size.

A set of survey notes is important as it forms the basis of all architectural projects. Survey notes are real dimensions measured in units: millimeters, centimeters, or meters (inches, feet, or yards).

This project involves considering the design of building components that we use every day. It needs to be understood at the scale of the city, from a map, to an elevation and door opening, through to the detail of what you touch, for example, the handle of a door.

Checklist

- Keep a photographic survey and observational drawings in parallel.

- Identify a datum (base line) to work from and check dimensions.

- Robust geometry and site lines will ensure dimensions can be triangulated (traversed).

- Keep dimensions and observational sketches.

- Check all horizontal and vertical dimensions carefully.

- Heights must be taken from a datum (base line).

- Ensure a selection of dimensions is double checked prior to leaving the site.

Process

Surveying any object or site requires a series of fixed points in order that detail measurements can be derived. It requires careful observation of the location at a series of scales. This step-by-step guide will teach you how to undertake a survey in relation to plan, section, and elevation.

1 Draw a measured grid in a sketchbook in pencil; for example, use a 1 cm (1/2 inch) grid. Use the entire sheet; it will act as a framework to work within.

2 Observe the object (or site) and note the key geometries that can be seen in your view. For example, key geometries, structures, features, and boundaries.

3 Construct a framework drawing in pencil, which quickly maps the object (or site) in plan. This drawing is not to scale, and will act as a base to add your dimensions. Observe carefully and ensure the elements drawn are proportional.

4 Measure the object (or site) and record these dimensions on the framework drawing. Use line weights and trace overlays to give the drawing clarity. Use a fine pen weight to add dimensions and thicker pen weights to express the plan.

5 Add notes and descriptions to your drawings that help you remember key details and dimensions. Observe complex areas of the survey and record in detail sketches.

6 Repeat the drawing for the section and elevation studies of the object (or site).

This exercise is about careful observation, drawing, and measuring. Use the grid to support your observational drawing. Draw lightly first and then make the line more definite when you are more confident.

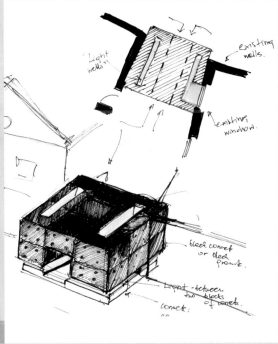

2.20

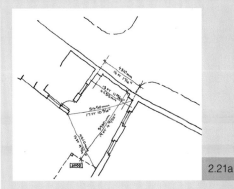

2.21a

2.21b

2.20

Project: New entrance
Location: Portsmouth, UK
Designer: Aleksandra Wojciak

These design sketches explore
the scale of the site and initial
ideas. The sketches are based
on the measurements taken
on the site and recorded in
survey drawings.

2.21a–2.21b

Project: Step by Step
Location: Survey
Architect: Nicola Crowson

These sketches are part of a
sequence that describes how
to construct a plan survey.
They illustrate the structural
grid, plan sketch, line weights,
and inclusion of dimensions.
Fixed points are noted on
the drawings; these act as a
baseline from which to take
accurate measurement.

Survey drawing equipment

- Sketchbook
- Architect's scale rule (30 cm or 12 inches)
- Tape measure
- Mechanical pencil 0.5 mm
- Fiber-tip pens (0.2, 0.5, 0.8 mm)
- Roll of sketch and trace paper

3.1

3 Orthographic Projection

Displaying a proposed piece of architecture as a series of drawings presents an interesting challenge. The information in the drawings needs to be both accurate and interconnected to tell the story of the building and communicate the proposed scheme clearly using a system that is universally recognized and understood. These drawings are 2D images that need to be read and interpreted as a 3D building or space.

Orthographic projection refers to a system of interrelated 2D views of a building. This system includes the views from above or a horizontal cross-section of a building (the plan), the views from the side of a building (the elevation), and the views of vertical "cuts" or cross-sections of the building (the section). These drawings can be collectively referred to as a "full set" and will include all floor plans, the roof plan, all elevations, and a series of vertical "cuts" that explain the internal and external relationships of the building.

The purpose of these drawings is to technically describe how to physically realize a conceptual idea. The plan, section, and elevation all relate to one another and depending on the conceptual idea of these drawings can be a starting point. Often, the plan is drawn first and section and elevations are then drawn alongside it. Using CAD software, the plans will be carefully drawn on different "layers" ensuring that the floor plan of the ground and subsequent floors align.

Reading plan, section and elevation drawings correctly is a skill. This chapter describes how the convention of plan, section, and elevation are used to describe architectural ideas and design buildings and structures.

3.1

Project: Thomas House
Location: Pencclawd, Wales
Architects: Hyde & Hyde

This section drawing shows the relationship between the site and the proposed Thomas House. The drawing explains the key aspects of the project, a building elevated over an uneven terrain that has been utilized to provide a ramped driveway. The section is represented in black with photorealistic materials applied in elevation.

Plans

A plan is an orthographic projection of a 3D object from the position of a horizontal plane through the object. In other words, a plan is a section viewed from above. To plan an architectural idea is to develop and organize its scheme. This is an important and iterative process when designing architecture, and the end product of this process is the plan drawing.

Architecture evolves as the plan of a scheme is drawn and redrawn again and again, perhaps shifting elements such as doors and openings, or changing descriptions of the space and its connections with any rooms around it. Creating the plan is the most volatile part of the design process. What starts as a diagram of spaces and shapes with associated functions becomes more refined as the design evolves.

Planning architecture requires an understanding and appreciation of the relationships between the different spaces within a proposed building or structure. Generating an overview of the whole building is the necessary first step towards this understanding. The overview drawing will be composed as a series of rooms and spaces that are connected by circulation (stairs, lifts, or corridors, for example).

Once the overview plan has been designed, the building's individual rooms need to be planned in detail by introducing furniture, doors, and other elements. As the individual plans of the rooms are worked out, the floor plan is likely to require adjustment as the relationship between the building, its rooms, their functions, and the use of materials, geometry, symmetry, and route are further developed.

3.2

Project: Chattock House
Location: Newport, Wales
Architect: John Pardey
Architects

The site for this house sits on the northern edge of the Newport Estuary in Pembrokeshire National Park, Wales. These plans locate the site of the house and provide information about the immediate context of the site by displaying the surrounding buildings and landscape. The larger plans show more details of the landscape around the house and the contours suggest the slope of the site.

os map @ 1:2500

extent of model

3.2

Drawing conventions

When drawing a plan, graphic conventions are used to describe the layout. Incorporating these conventions removes the need to include any accompanying text to further explain the drawing.

Variations in line thickness are used to indicate different degrees of solidity or permanence in the plan. A thicker line suggests more permanence or a denser material (so might be used to signify a masonry wall), and a thinner line suggests a more temporary quality or a lighter material (so might be used to suggest a temporary piece of furniture).

Finally, a plan drawing should always display a north point as this allows an understanding of the proposed building's relationship to its site and orientation and how sunlight will affect its different spaces.

Drawing conventions should be acknowledged, and plan drawings need to be consistent in their use of them. However, some architects may adopt a more idiosyncratic approach to their application of symbols and the types of information included in their drawings, which will create a distinctive, if not universal, practice style.

Types of plan

An architectural scheme will require a range of plan "types" to be created. A ground plan is a horizontal cut through a building (it cuts through the building's walls, windows, and openings) drawn at approximately 1200m (1312 yards) above the floor plane. A ground plan reveals the connections between inside and outside spaces, between internal rooms and layouts, and between the materials from which the building is made.

The ground floor plan should show the entrance to the building and its relationship to the exterior spaces and gardens. Other level floor plans, such as first or second floor plans, will clearly indicate staircases and connections between the building's levels. In cases where the floor plan is repetitive, for example in a housing or office block, then only one indicative plan may be shown to suggest the general layout of the building.

The roof plan should indicate the slope of the roof and its overhang on the walls. It may be shown separately or it may be incorporated in the site plan.

A location plan will be used to display the building within the context of its site or surroundings. It should clearly describe the proposed building's location in relationship to any surrounding important geographical or physical features such as local roads or important civic buildings.

A site plan will present a description of the building in the context of its site, and it should include surrounding buildings and other significant routes, paths, trees, or surrounding planting. A site plan shows these elements in more detail than a location plan. The site plan may be combined with the ground plan.

3.3a–3.3b

**Project: Tianjin EcoCity Ecology and Planning Museums
Location: Tianjin, China
Architect: Steven Holl Architects**

This plan is formed around a rectangular volume that has been carved away. Within the drawing, you can read the room arrangement due to the codes used. The inclusion of staircases, lifts, furniture, and labels ensures the clarity of information.

The section drawing describes the relationship between various galleries within the museum blocks. The section reveals an ocean ecology gallery, which is cut into the ground and connects the two buildings.

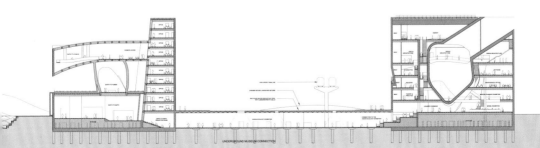

Aligning plans

It is crucial that all types of plans for a particular building or scheme align with one another. When creating freehand plans and developing your scheme, it is useful to draw each one on tracing paper as these can be laid over one another to ensure that they all align.

In CAD software, the floor plans are drawn on top of one another to ensure that they fully align. There are also facilities within CAD programs to repeat floor plans and to read them simultaneously. Essentially, the drawings exist as a series of layers within the program and each floor plan will be drawn on a different layer. This allows plans to be reproduced and altered quickly.

It is also important to ensure that floor plans are all aligned with the north point (or as near as possible to it), and all floor plans should be presented in the same orientation on a sheet to avoid any confusion when they are read together.

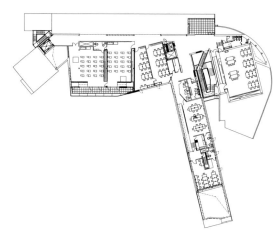

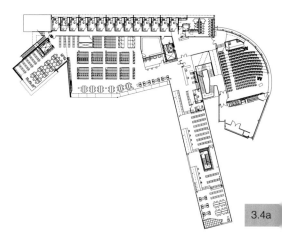

3.4a

3.4a–3.4b

Project: School of Art and Art History, University of Iowa
Location: Iowa, USA
Architect: Steven Holl Architects

This building is a hybrid structure of open edges and an open center. Flat or curved planes are slotted together in hinged sections. Flexible spaces open out from studios in warm weather, and the main horizontal passages become meeting places. The series of plans show the relationship of the different floor plans and also the relationship to the site and the surrounding landscape.

3.4b

3.5a–3.5b

Project: Conceptual scheme
Location: Atlas Mountains,
Morocco
Designers: Joshua Kievenaar
and Natasha Butler

The concept for these section drawings is a journey. They focus on key aspects that help us to understand our experience through the drawings; for example, the time of day is demonstrated through shadows. The section cut remains white, which allows us to focus on the view beyond; this view gives us an understanding of scale by showing people and materiality.

3.5a

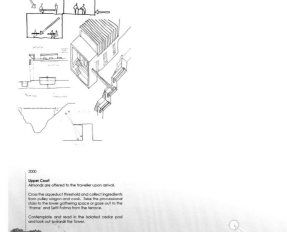

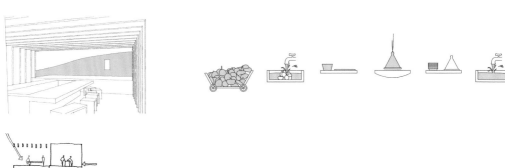

2000

Upper Court
Almonds are offered to the traveller upon arrival.

Cross the aqueduct threshold and collect ingredients
from pulley wagon and cook. Take the processional
stairs to the lower gathering space or gaze out to the
'Frame' and Setti Fatma from the terrace.

Contemplate and read in the isolated cedar pod
and look out towards the Tower.

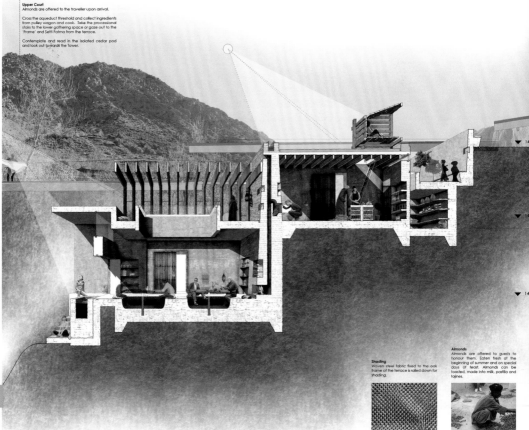

Shading
Woven steel fabric fixed to the oak
frame of the terrace is rolled down for
shading.

Almonds
Almonds are offered to guests to
honour them. Eaten fresh at the
beginning of summer and on special
days of feast. Almonds can be
toasted, made into milk, pastilla and
tajines.

3.5b

Sections

A section drawing is an orthographic projection of a 3D object from the position of a vertical plane through the object. In other words, it is a vertical cut through a building. A section drawing is one of the most useful and revealing drawings in the design and description of a building. As with all 2D drawings, a section is an abstract representation. It would be impractical and impossible to actually slice through a building and reveal its internal connections, so a useful analogy is to consider cutting through something that is possible to slice. For example, if you cut a piece of fruit, such as an apple, it will become immediately apparent that its skin is very thin and its flesh is relatively solid and dense; but if you slice an orange, you will expose a thicker skin protecting a softer fruit inside.

Section drawings communicate the connection between the inside and the outside of a building and the relationships between the building's rooms. They can also display the thickness of the building's walls and their relationship to internal elements such as the roof, the external boundary walls, gardens, and other spaces.

Without accompanying section drawings, the building plans can only suggest spatial arrangements. Once the section drawings are read alongside the plans, the heights of ceilings, doors and windows, double-height spaces or mezzanine decks can be described and explained. Together, the section and plan drawings allow the 3D picture of the building to be better understood.

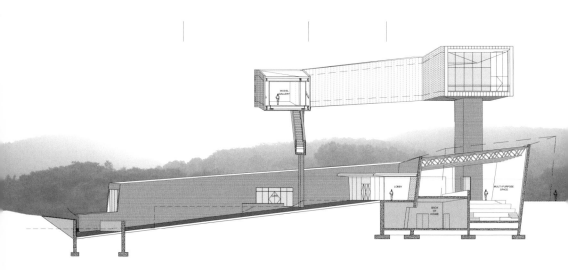

3.6a

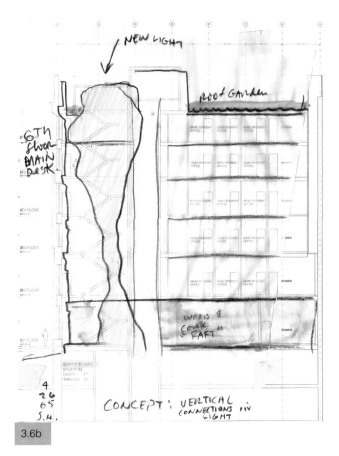

3.6b

3.6a–3.6b

Project: New York University
Location: New York, USA
Architect: Steven Holl
Architects

This concept section drawing
was produced as part of a
design scheme for the
interior renovation of an 1890
corner building at the New
York University. The concept
organizes new spaces around
light and the phenomenological
properties of materials. A new
stair shaft below a new skylight
joins a six-level building
vertically with a shifting porosity
of light and shadow that
change seasonally.

Cross-section

A cross-section is a vertical
plane cut through an object,
building, or space in the
same way a floor plan is
cut horizontally. This plane
is known as the "cutting
plane" or "section plane".
The section is often shown
as a bold line, rendered black
or left white. The choice of
where to cut the section and
how to represent it is always
dependent on the key
message that you wish
to communicate.

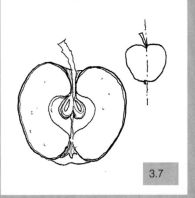

3.7

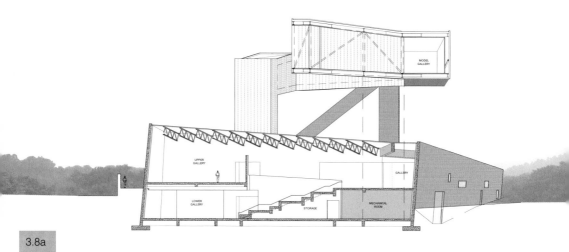

3.8a

Long and short sections

As with architectural plans, simply producing a single section drawing of a proposed building is insufficient. The different section drawings should be taken from the most interesting, complex, or unusual parts of the plan and will explain an aspect of the building that cannot be understood from the plan drawings alone. A long section drawing is created from the longest part of the plan to show the interrelationships between the areas within it. A short section drawing is taken from the narrowest part of the plan.

All section drawings are individually labeled (the standard convention is to use AA, BB, CC and so on for each one), and the corresponding labels are displayed on the plan to show where the section line is cut. Section drawings are also labeled with their orientation points (north, east, etc.) so that they can be read in conjunction with the elevation drawings.

3.8a

Project: Nanjing Museum of Art and Architecture
Location: Nanjing, China
Architect: Steven Holl Architects

This long section drawing describes the relationship between the various galleries on the museum's lower block, and storage and plant hidden underneath. There is another building element raised above the houses and model gallery.

Sections and rendering

Rendering techniques are used on presentation drawings to allow clients to understand the qualities of the space (technical sections show construction information). Rendering sections by hand or on the computer allows designers to convey tone, texture, and reality within the drawings. Shadow casting can also be used to add atmosphere to orthographic projections. Such techniques give the drawing a sense of depth and interior quality; these are demonstrated on page 96.

Sections and other representations

Other forms of representation can be combined with section drawings to create useful interpretations of a building. For example, a sectional perspective drawing combines a 2D section drawing with a 3D perspective drawing. This can create a powerful image that suggests how the internal spaces within the building can be used.

Physical models that are built in the form of a sectional cut can also allow the inside of a proposed building to be better understood. Creating a series of sectional models can fully explain a complex scheme and its relationship to the surrounding landscape or environment. Hinged sectional models can be opened and closed to reveal the internal spaces in a building.

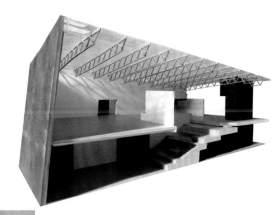

3.8b

3.8b

Project: Nanjing Museum of Art and Architecture
Location: Nanjing, China
Architect: Steven Holl Architects

Models are very effective means of exploring the sectional idea of a building. They can be photographed to create a series of views (shown in this image as a perspective view into the space and a long sectional view). This sectional model describes how light enters into the building and the connections between the various floor levels of the interior spaces.

SOUTH ELEVATION

white render
cedar cladding panels
timber sliding screens
powder coated aluminium windows
coloured render
glazed balustrade
standing seam zinc roof
rendered chimney
garage set within hillside

3.9

3.9

Project: Chattock House
Location: Newport, Wales
Architects: John Pardey
Architects

This drawing describes the west
elevation of the scheme and
also provides heights to relate
the building to its landscape
levels. Figures in the drawing
allow the relative scale of the
building to be understood, and
the shading suggests shadow
from overhanging elements of
the roof.

Elevations

In architectural terms, an elevation
drawing describes the vertical plane of a
building or space. An elevation drawing
can be an external view (for example, of a
building or street), or an internal one (for
example, of a room).

The elevation is the interface between
the inside and the outside of a building.
Buildings can be designed from the outside
to the inside by using the elevation to
generate the internal plan. However, most
architects usually begin the design process
with the plan, and the elevation drawings
are created in response to it. This means
that elevation drawings are often drawn
and redrawn as the plan evolves so that
design decisions can be understood and
connected to the external form.

Elevation drawings are normally labeled
with the direction that the elevation faces
(so the south elevation is south facing, the
north elevation is north facing and so on).
This connects the elevations directly to the
orientation of the plan, and it immediately
allows an understanding of how the sunlight
will affect the building over the course of the
day and with the change of the seasons.

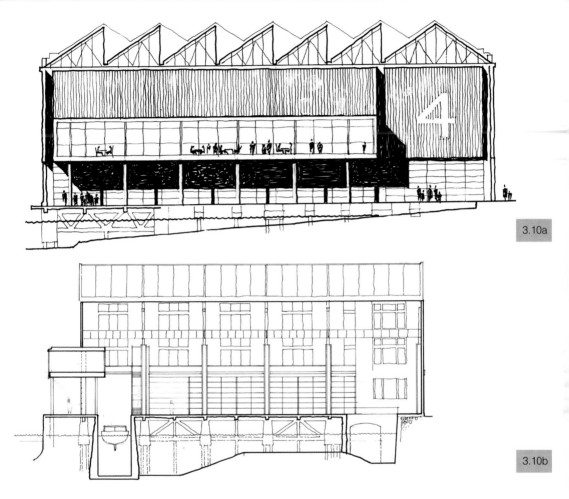

3.10a

3.10b

3.10a–3.10b

Project: HM Dockyard
Location: Portsmouth
Architects: Sir Colin Stansfield
Smith and John Pardey

This is an elevation drawing
of an existing building and
proposed scheme. It is a hand-
drawn elevation that reads as
a sketch image. However, it is
carefully drawn and considered
using a variety of line weights
to describe the different
aspects of the architecture;
there is a hierarchy of line,
which is evident in the drawing.

Elevation and context

The most important aspect of an elevation
is that it forms the "skin" of the building. As
such, a building's elevations need to relate
to their context or surrounding environment.
This requires the architect to develop a
solid understanding of any surrounding
buildings and aspects of the existing
architecture (such as the materials they
use, or their scale, massing, and height),
and the rhythm of a proposed location. All
this will provide clues for an appropriate
architectural response and suggest how
a proposed design might respond to
its context. Drawings of any proposed
buildings should incorporate the elevation
views of the surrounding architecture so
that the scale of the proposed building can
be understood.

Context doesn't need to be thought of as
a limiting factor. In fact, it helps to locate
the architecture. However, the choice or
precedent of scale, mass, or materials
used will affect aspects of the elevation.
For example, if the windows are pushed
back within the building's elevation, there
will be a greater sense of shadow around
the window openings. Such features can
all be explored in elevation drawings and,
in doing so, help the architect to consider
different possibilities and variations before
deciding which approach or solution is
most appropriate.

A well-designed elevation will respond to
and complement its location and context
in terms of the use of materials, massing,
and scale. As a piece of design, it needs
to be balanced and well proportioned,
but equally, it will also need to respond to
the requirements of the building layout,
with appropriate openings for views and
access. The elevation needs to mediate
between these two challenging aspects of
architectural design.

3.11

Project: Urban Acupuncture
Location: Istanbul, Turkey
Architect: Adam Parsons

This conceptual scheme for
an area of housing in Istanbul,
Turkey is part of a strategy
called "Urban Acupuncture".
The scheme is inspired by the
site's dramatic context within
the city and uses this as the
concept behind the drawings.
This elevation drawing shows
the proposal in elevation and
uses photographic images
as the background to give a
realistic impression of the city.

Drawing conventions

Architectural drawings use a distinct language of convention systems that are used universally to enable the information they contain to be easily understood with little or no need for additional explanatory text.

Scale

One of the most useful conventions is the incorporation of scale. Ideally, the title of an architectural drawing should describe the scale used, but if not a measuring rule can be drawn at the side of the drawing as a reference. Information about a drawing's scale provides the viewer with a better understanding of the scheme's proportions and helps to communicate the proposal's information clearly.

3.12

Project: St Faiths
Location: Havant, UK
Designer: Joshua Kievenaar and Natasha Butler

This plan shows the interior of a room proposed for a conceptual project called "St Faiths". It explores the relationship between the plan cut and the qualities of the interior. The drawing is purposely focused on one room only, so you only see the interior line of the plan. Photomontages of people and shadows are mapped onto the drawings to give a sense of scale and place.

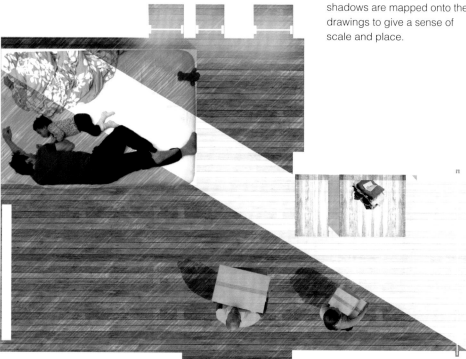

3.12

Orientation

A north point that indicates the orientation of the building is an essential aspect of a site or ground plan. The direction and flow of natural light into a space and how it is modified are important considerations for architects. Understanding the building's orientation will also explain many aspects of the internal layout and spatial organization shown in the plan.

Line thickness

In architectural drawings, the thickness of the drawn line has a meaning that communicates a design intention. The general rule in an architectural drawing is: the thicker the line the denser the material, or the more permanent the object being described. Thinner lines are used for furniture and variable elements in the plan; these are also often used to communicate additional information about the scheme. Thick lines will be more legible and read as a primary layer of information, whilst the thinner lines read as a secondary layer.

When creating a section drawing, the standard convention is to make the lines thicker at the point where the building has been "cut". This distinction allows the viewer to identify where the cut has been made in relation to the plan.

Staircases

Staircases exist between two or more floor levels, and they need to be communicated on a plan drawing. The standard convention is that the staircase is drawn as a solid line up to 1200mm (approximately 47 inches) above floor level, and as a dotted line above this level. An arrow is used to indicate the direction of movement up a staircase.

Materials

Materials and their intended use in a building are also communicated in architectural drawings, specifically the plan drawing, which will explain layout and spatial organization. Different materials are denoted by variations in shading and hatching conventions.

Symbols

Symbols are frequently used in architectural drawings as a form of shorthand to describe the position and location of elements in the building. This shorthand is used by all members of the construction team from building contractors, suppliers, and installers to architects and designers.

When creating a freehand line drawing, these symbols can be generated using a template. If creating digital drawings, CAD software programs incorporate object libraries, allowing the user to select the relevant symbol and position it on their drawing. Recognized symbols include pieces of furniture (to suggest internal layout), bathroom fittings (such as a bath or sink), and kitchen fittings (to show the location of the sink or cooker).

Drawing categories

The various stages in the development of an architectural design have different categories of drawings associated with them. These categories include: feasibility study drawings, presentation drawings, working drawings, and specialized drawings, all of which will be discussed in more depth in the following sections.

Feasibility study drawings

The first of these stages is a feasibility study; this is a preliminary study undertaken to determine and document a project's viability. The results of this study are used to determine whether or not to proceed with the project. At this stage, the site, plan drawings, elevations, and relevant section drawings will all be required. As the scheme develops, the range of drawings necessary to fulfill the different information requirements increases. For example, further sets of drawings will be produced to request permission to build, or for public consultation exercises.

Presentation drawings

Presentation drawings are normally intended for a client audience. As such, they need to be persuasive as they must present the strongest and most convincing aspects of the scheme design. These drawings need to have impact, be accessible, be easy to understand, and communicate the scheme concepts clearly. At the stage of public consultation or planning, a set of presentation drawings is needed to explain the relationship of the scheme to its immediate context and the impact the building may have on its site.

Working drawings

Further stages of the design's development will have more detailed sets of drawings associated with them. The drawings that are used to build a piece of architecture are described as a "working set". These will include plans, sections, and elevations, as well as detailed drawings and sections that explain room layout and specifications, which describe materials and other aspects of construction.

3.13

The details within this range of drawings will provide information about the structure of the building and construction elements such as the relationship between the walls and the foundation; the walls and the internal floors, and the walls and the roof. Any project-specific or specialized details will also be included; these may be bespoke aspects of the architecture that need to be built in a specific way, or an unusual use of a particular building material.

Coordinated production information (CPI) is an acknowledged scale system that is applied to working drawings. Different drawing types will be created in different scale ratios. For example, exterior information is produced at 1:100 or 1:50 scale (depending on the size of the building); interior information will be provided at 1:50 or 1:20 scale; and the detailed drawings will be provided at 1:5, 1:10 and 1:2 scale (see page 37).

Working drawings are issued at the point when the scheme is agreed. But on-site, as problems or issues crop up, revisions to the drawings may be made. Availability of materials, changes in programming, or an alteration in the client's requirements may mean that alterations are necessary. If, however, one drawing is revised, then all other drawings that relate to it must also be amended in order to ensure that the drawings still work in conjunction with one another to provide a full set of information.

Specialized drawings

Specialized drawings allow the manufacture of particular, perhaps bespoke, items by a supplier. Structural, mechanical, and environmental engineers will also issue specialized drawings that respond to specific design problems or issues.

3.13

Project: Oxford Brookes University
Location: Oxford, UK
Architect: Design Engine

This rendered view shows a series of bridges crossing a main circulation space. The use of a computer model allows information on materials' surfaces, light and reflection to be emphasized in order to give a sense of reality. The glass bridges provide a flash of color to the interior and emphasizes the verticality of the space.

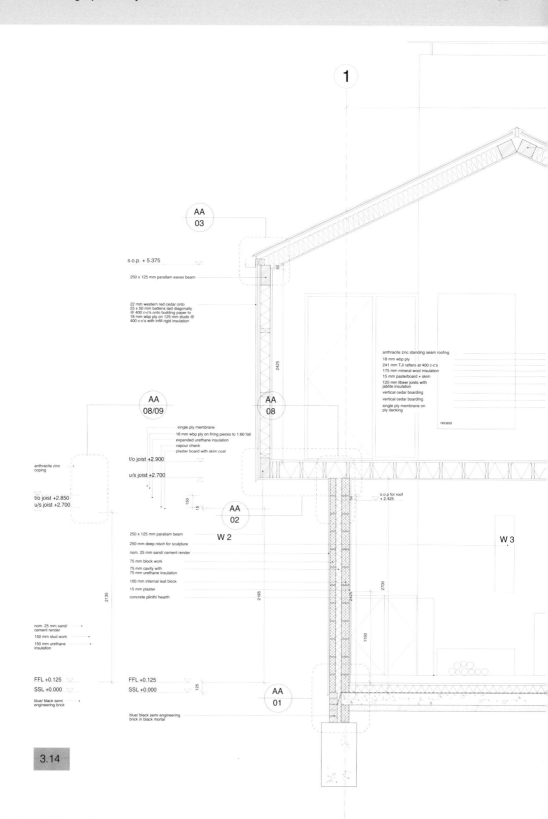

s.o.p. + 5.375

250 x 125 mm parallam eaves beam

22 mm western red cedar onto
25 x 50 mm battens laid diagonally
@ 400 c-c's onto building paper to
18 mm wbp ply on 125 mm studs @
400 c-c's with infill rigid insulation

AA 03

AA 08

anthracite zinc standing seam roofing
18 mm wbp ply
241 mm TJI rafters at 400 c-c's
175 mm mineral wool insulation
15 mm pasterboard + skim
125 mm tibeer joists with
jablite insulation
vertical cedar boarding
vertical cedar boarding
single ply membrane on
ply decking

recess

AA 08/09

single ply membrane
18 mm wbp ply on firing pieces to 1:60 fall
expanded urethane insulation
vapour check
plaster board with skim coat

anthracite zinc
coping

t/o joist +2.900

u/s joist +2.700

t/o joist +2.850
u/s joist +2.700

s.o.p for roof
+ 2.425

AA 02

250 x 125 mm parallam beam

250 mm deep nisch for sculpture

nom. 25 mm sand/ cement render

75 mm block work

75 mm cavity with
75 mm urethane insulation

100 mm internal leaf block

15 mm plaster

concrete plinth/ hearth

W 2

W 3

nom. 25 mm sand/
cement render

150 mm stud work

150 mm urethane
insulation

FFL +0.125

SSL +0.000

blue/ black semi
engineering brick

FFL +0.125

SSL +0.000

blue/ black semi engineering
brick in black mortar

AA 01

3.14

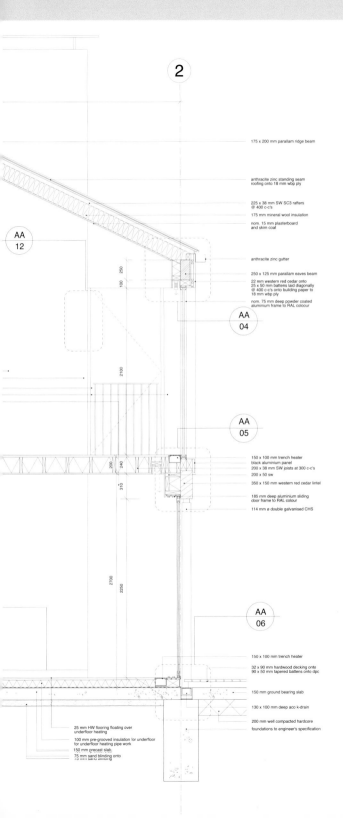

2

175 x 200 mm parallam ridge beam

anthracite zinc standing seam
roofing onto 18 mm wbp ply

225 x 38 mm SW SC3 rafters
@ 400 c-c's

175 mm mineral wool insulation

nom. 15 mm plasterboard
and skim coat

AA 12

anthracite zinc gutter

250 x 125 mm parallam eaves beam

22 mm western red cedar onto
25 x 50 mm battens laid diagonally
@ 400 c-c's onto building paper to
18 mm wbp ply

nom. 75 mm deep powder coated
aluminium frame to RAL colour

AA 04

AA 05

150 x 100 mm trench heater
black aluminium panel

200 x 38 mm SW joists at 300 c-c's

200 x 50 sw

350 x 150 mm western red cedar lintel

185 mm deep aluminium sliding
door frame to RAL colour

114 mm ø double galvanised CHS

AA 06

150 x 100 mm trench heater

32 x 90 mm hardwood decking onto
90 x 50 mm tapered battens onto dpc

150 mm ground bearing slab

130 x 100 mm deep aco k-drain

200 mm well compacted hardcore

foundations to engineer's specification

25 mm HW flooring floating over
underfloor heating

100 mm pre-grooved insulation for underfloor
for underfloor heating pipe work

150 mm precast slab

75 mm sand blinding onto

3.14

**Project: Duckett House
Location: New Forest, UK
Architect: John Pardey
Architects**

Every design project will require
a set of detailed drawings
that explain the building's
assembly and construction.
This set of drawings forms part
of a package of information
designed to assist in the
construction of the building.
The package will include
detailed information about
size and dimension of fixtures,
fittings, and any specialized
components needed.

Case study: Salvador Dalí Museum, USA by HOK

Architects have to use quite complex drawings to describe large cultural buildings. This is because the site may need to be explained with a location plan. Plans may be large in scale, covering internal space, external gardens, and public squares. Large-scale buildings also have complex service systems, which may be modeled using BIM (Building Information Modeling, which uses 3D software). BIM allows the building to be modeled before construction work starts.

The Salvador Dalí Museum in St Petersburg, Florida was designed by HOK, a large international multidisciplinary practice in the USA. The museum, completed in 2011, is a three-storey building that sits on the waterfront. Its distinctive architectural form has created a dramatic, sculptural building, which echoes Dalí's work. It houses many of the Spanish surrealist's paintings, drawings, photographs, and objets d'arts.

During the design of the museum, a range of drawing techniques was used to explore the concept as well as the technical details. Externally, the building needed to be distinctive and to connect to the surrounding landscape; internally, it needed to create a space where light and humidity could be controlled in order to protect the art exhibits.

HOK used BIM to visualize the complex geometries of the museum's concept. The fluid shapes could not have been developed using conventional 2D drawing platforms. The use of a 3D model allows the geometries of the idea to be tested.

The building is composed mainly of two elements: a glass geodesic form, described as the "enigma", which is over 20 meters high with a 13-meter high, glazed sculptural form called the "igloo". This is formed from over 1,000 undulating faceted glass panels, all individually shaped to fit together. Using BIM meant that the unique shapes of the glazing were manufactured efficiently.

The building consists of an exhibition space, with large galleries for both temporary and permanent collections connected by a sculptural gallery. It also includes a library that opens to the exterior balcony, a museum store, an auditorium, offices, a café with indoor and outdoor seating, and a series of outdoor spaces. The main interior features are a "poured-in-place" and a concrete spiral staircase, which encourages visitors to explore the galleries above.

The collection also has to be sheltered from potential Category 5 hurricane winds and storm surges, so it has been designed within a protective environment called a "treasure box".

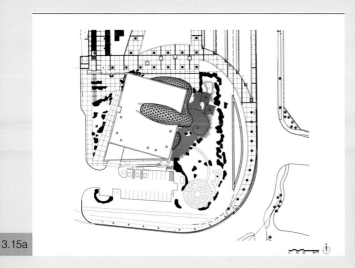

3.15a

3.15d

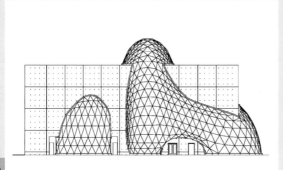

3.15b

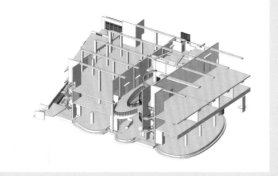

3.15c

3.15a–3.15d

Project: Salvador Dalí Museum
Location: Florida, USA
Architects: HOK

These drawings and images show the linear form of the Dalí Museum. The site plan (image 3.15a) describes the relationship of the building form to the surrounding space and indicates landscape treatment.

The complex shapes and sculptural forms of the exhibition spaces, have been developed on computer and the cutaway images reveal the structure of the building (images 3.15b and 3.15c).

A series of dynamic sculptural elements, for example the main staircase, refines the interior as it casts a dramatic shadow within the glazed atrium space (image 3.15d).

Project: Orthographic projection

This church competition proposed a scheme inspired by site geology and by the idea of gathering around light. The church is designed around a central hearth, reached by a tunnel starting beneath a bell tower; from this, chapels radiate.

The drawings are rendered to show light, shadow, and material quality within the interior. Shadow casting can be used to add a reality and atmosphere to orthographic projections. Light reveals texture and depth of surfaces, or, by its absence, shade, shadow, and silhouette.

Process

Rendering provides an opportunity to show the pattern and texture of the building elements. This step-by-step guide shows how to apply line weights to your drawings, test rendering techniques and the process of casting shadows (sciagraphy).

1 Create a set of plans and sections in pencil at a scale of 1:50. Use tracing to project from a plan drawing to a section drawing.

2 Add line weights to identify the hierarchy of information. In pen, use a thick line (0.8 mm) to represent the section cut, thin lines (0.3 mm) represent steps and edges, or dashed lines identify volumes above.

3 In plan, draw a slanting line at 45 degrees towards the upper-right corner of the drawing. In section/elevation, this line slants to the lower right. Draw the shadow length along the 45-degree construction line at two-thirds of the actual shadow length.

4 Use soft pencil or graphite to render the shadows within the construction lines. A shadow can be rendered as a hatched line, solid render, or a series of marks. Observe shadows around windows, and recesses in walls and projections.

5 Use a range of shading strengths and techniques to give texture to the drawing and to convey materiality.

6 Include people to give the drawings a sense of scale. Try representing people as silhouettes, outlines, or as collaged elements.

7 Scan the drawings and print on high-quality cartridge paper. This gives a hand-drawn quality. If no resizing takes place, they will remain scale drawings.

Sciagraphy

The direction of light in orthographic drawing follows a single principle, which aims to represent shadows cast by a simple cube. Skiagraphy is the technique of shadow projection made by an object onto plans and sections providing the orthographic view with a sense of depth. The main angle used in shadow projection is 45 degrees; alternatives include projections at 30 and 60 degrees.

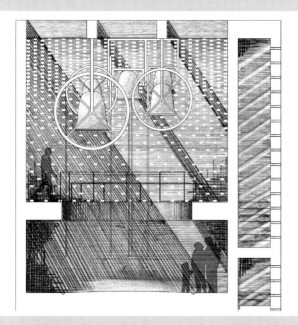

3.16a

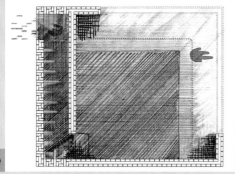

3.16b

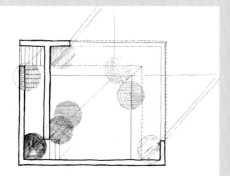

3.16c

3.16a–3.16c

Project: The Sacred Tree, Absent Tree, and The Monument
Location: Conceptual
Designers: Paul Cashin and Simon Drayson

This sequence of images introduces the process of adding rendering to orthographic drawings to provide texture. The final rendered drawings are created by a combination of pencil-rendered techniques, the plan cut has been left white to further emphasize the interior surfaces. This has been overlaid with shadow casting to give a reality and to reveal the material qualities.

Equipment you will need
- Mechanical pencil 0.5 mm
- Architect's scale rule (12" or 30 cm)
- A selection of soft graphite sketching pencils
- Roll of sketch and trace paper
- A set of technical pens
- Cartridge or watercolor paper
- Set square/45-degree angle
- T-square or small drawing board

4.1

4 Three-dimensional (3D) Images

It can sometimes be difficult to read 2D architectural drawings because certain drawing conventions can appear like a specialized code. 2D architectural drawings are often attempting to represent 3D spaces or places, which is not always easy. 3D images can make the interpretation of a building so much easier; they create an impression of a building that is immediately accessible.

Each of the different 3D drawing techniques explored in this chapter can provide a different way to view the building. Perspective drawings allow the view from a particular standpoint, and axonometric and isometric drawings create 3D forms from a particular point, which can be viewed in the same way as a model. The choice of view is the most important consideration when deciding which image type is relevant.

Images that are 3D create an impression of what it might be like to occupy or work in a building, and they can be combined with other 2D drawings to give a convincing overall impression of a scheme or project.

4.1

Project: Kolkata Living Steel competition
Location: Kolkata, India
Architect: Piercy & Company

These architects recognize that contemporary housing rarely deviates from the accepted model of sealed cellular spaces. This CAD image presents a perspective model of the scheme. The bird's-eye view is taken from the second-floor level, and it allows an understanding of the relationship between the buildings and the street, and gives a glimpse of the rooftop gardens. Shadow and texture give the image a sense of reality.

4.2

4.3

Perspective

Although perspective images usually offer a true impression of a space, there are distortions in perspective that can make the impossible appear possible.

Perspective images can be open to interpretation and manipulation by the architect or artist, who will decide what is and what is not seen, and where the perspective's viewpoint is taken from.

Standpoint (Station point)

All perspective images are taken from a particular view, standpoint, or station point. The standpoint will determine everything about the view that is described. It is usually taken at a standard eye-level height, but it can be manipulated so that the view is altered. A bird's-eye view, for example, is a standpoint from above, producing a perspective that reads as if one is flying over the scheme. A worm's-eye view produces a contrasting perspective, looking at the scheme from underneath.

4.2

Project: Nelson-Atkins Museum of Art
Location: Kansas City, USA
Architect: Steven Holl Architects

This competition-winning addition to the Nelson-Atkins Museum of Art consists of five interconnecting structures. Traversing from the existing building across a sculpture park, the five built "lenses" form new spaces and angles of vision creating new experiences of the existing museum. This interior sketch explores the quality of light inside the gallery space.

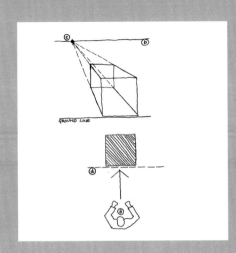

GROUND LINE

4.4

Perspective

a **Standpoint**: the point from which a viewer is related to the object/figure in perspective.

b **Horizon**: the eye level from which the viewer is looking.

c **Vanishing point**: the point at which lines converge within the perspective.

d **Picture plane**: the imaginary plane corresponding to the surface of a picture.

4.3

Project: Institute for
Contemporary Art
Location: Virginia
Commonwealth University,
Richmond, USA
Architect: Steven Holl
Architects

The Institute for Contemporary Art is organized into four galleries, each with a different character. This interior sketch explores the quality of light inside the gallery space. It gives a sense of perspective, and it is drawn in pencil and rendered with watercolor.

The picture plane

A picture plane is the imaginary flat surface located between the viewer's standpoint and the object being viewed. Ordinarily, a vertical plane is perpendicular to the horizontal projection of the line of sight to the object's point of interest. The nearer the picture plane is to the object, the larger the image will be. If the picture plane is farther away, the resulting image will be smaller.

The picture plane is a concept borrowed from fine art. Albrecht Dürer (1471–1528) developed a grid through which a 3D scene could be depicted with accuracy on a flat plane.

By positioning the grid close to the subject matter, drawing a similar grid pattern onto the paper, using the lines on the grid, and the corresponding lines on the paper as a sort of "map", the artist could transfer what they saw onto the paper surface. Using the grid helped ensure that all aspects of the subject remained in proportion.

4.5

The vanishing point

Perspective views can be single-, two-, or three-point representations. These points correspond to the number of points at which all lines in the drawing appear to converge. Each point of convergence is called the "vanishing point".

A single-point perspective drawing has a central vanishing point, which will exaggerate the sense of a space's depth. Single-point perspective is often used for interior drawings. Two-point perspective images are often used to describe smaller buildings in a space or street context. Three-point perspective images are used to describe larger buildings and their surrounding environment and context.

4.5

**Project: Story Telling Centre
Location: Ourika Valley,
Morocco
Designers: Toby Richardson
and Sam Sclater-Brooks**

This scheme uses the connection with the landscape as its focus. An image of the landscape has been used in the distance to give perspective. This has been overlaid with hand drawing and collage to add scale and materiality. The perspective was generated in CAD to create a frame on which the collage is based.

The horizon

The eye-level line in a perspective drawing is referred to as the "horizon". The point of horizon is normally about 1.6 meters (approximately 5 feet) above floor level, but this can be altered to obtain different viewpoints (such as a bird's-eye view).

Sketch perspective

To sketch in perspective first observe and study a view, and then draw an image that accurately renders that view. This requires some consideration of the vanishing point and the horizon. Sketch perspective is a useful tool to quickly communicate a realistic impression of an existing space or to suggest a design concept.

Constructed perspective

A constructed perspective is a freehand drawing created from plan, section, and elevation information. To create a constructed perspective, it is first necessary to decide the standpoint of the drawing and to then use the section and elevation drawings to suggest the details of heights of spaces and openings—such as doors and windows. There are important principles when creating a perspective image:

● all lines must converge into the vanishing point;

● figures should get smaller as they move towards the center of the image and towards the vanishing point;

● space and depth must be maintained in the image to reinforce the illusion of the perspective and its suggested reality.

4.6

4.6

Project: Student housing scheme
Location: Rotterdam, The Netherlands
Designer: Jeremy Davies

This perspective sketch uses color to animate the building's elevation. Scaled figures are also used to give a sense of reality and activity to the space around the building.

Axonometric drawings

An axonometric drawing (also known as a plan oblique drawing) is produced from a plan elevation drawing and is the easiest of the 3D projections to create.

Axonometric drawings are a true scale drawing unlike perspective and, as such, allow an overall aerial view of an object. The advantage of an axonometric drawing is that it allows an understanding of both the plan and the building's internal or external elevations.

Architectural historian Auguste Choisy (1841–1909) first used axonometric drawings in the nineteenth century and numerous influential twentieth-century artists and architects have employed them ever since, including the Russian constructivists, Kazimir Malevich (1878–1935) and El Lissitzky (1890–1941), as well as De Stijl members such as Gerrit Rietveld (1888–1964). For these artists and architects, axonometric drawings connected very well with their avant-garde architectural and artistic style. For example, the axonometric technique complemented the De Stijl movement's cubist forms of architecture. Today, architects, such as Zaha Hadid, continue to favor axonometric techniques as a signature style of expression.

4.7

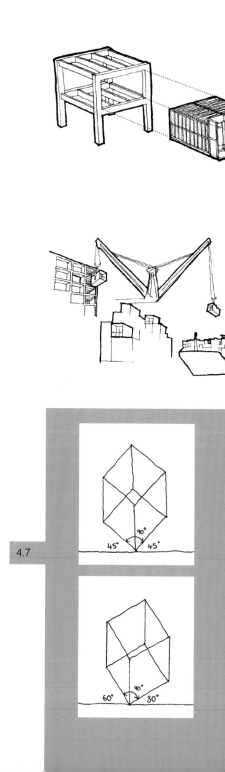

4.8

Making axonometric drawings

Axonometric drawings can be created using the following steps:

- Rotate the scale plan, section, or elevation drawing to 45 degrees from the horizontal. Thirty or 60 degrees from the horizontal can also be used if emphasis is required on the top surface.

- Project vertical lines from the rotated scale drawing. All vertical lines remain parallel to one another.

- Measure vertical heights onto the drawing. The scale of the drawing will remain true.

- From the vertical measurements, draft parallel lines to the 45-degree (or 30-degree) rotation. All parallel lines remain parallel.

4.8
_____

Project: Urban Acupuncture
Location: Istanbul, Turkey
Designer: Adam Parsons

This isometric drawing is an exploded 3D view that reveals how a series of bedroom pods slot together. Isometric is a form of axonometric projection in which the view can appear distorted. The projection is created around the vertical axis and uses 30 degrees from the horizontal. Measurements are transposed onto the drawing as opposed to rotating the orthographic drawings.

Producing an axonometric drawing

To produce an axonometric drawing, you need to redraw or recreate a plan view at an angle of 45 degrees to the horizontal. The plan needs to be oriented so that the right view is achieved axonometrically, for example, there may be a particular elevation aspect of the building that needs to be represented. At this new orientation, the plan is redrawn and all lines are projected vertically. All measures remain real and are taken from the elevation and section drawings.

Once the overall form or framework of the axonometric drawing is achieved, it is then possible to cut away sections to reveal details of the building's interior or its construction. Axonometric drawings allow a simultaneous view of the inside and outside of a building.

Exploded axonometric drawings

Exploded axonometric drawings can explain a concept or idea as a series of visual components. This drawing type is useful to explain a complex idea or concept, and it describes how each of the design's components could be assembled together. Perspective and isometric drawings can also be exploded.

4.9

Project: Clone House
Location: Conceptual
Architect: CJ Lim/Studio 8 Architects

The conceptual Clone House comprises of four identical rooms and questions the idea of everyday existence by suggesting a variety of permutations and configurations. This exploded perspective drawing separates aspects of the design into a series of images, which identify different elements of the structure such as roofs, walls, and the staircase.

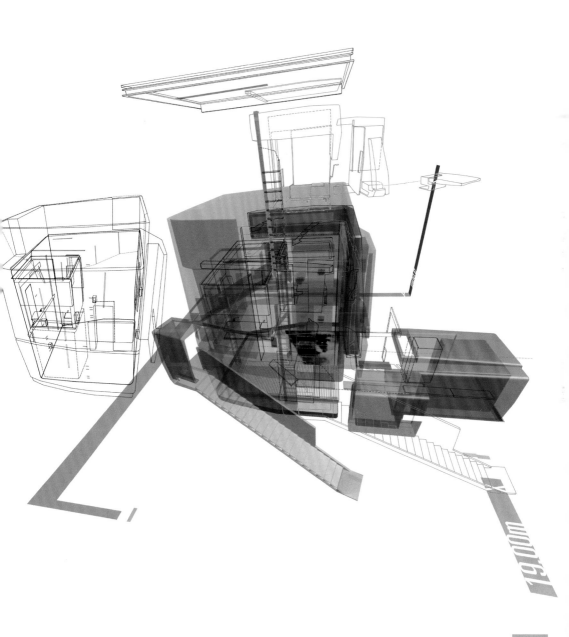

4.9

Isometric drawings

Isometric drawings offer similar 3D views to those of axonometric drawings. However, these drawings attempt to make the very technical representation of an axonometric view slightly more accessible and more of a perspective representation.

Isometric images are useful as they place less emphasis on the vertical aspect of the view. They are also easy to interpret because there is a lower eye level in the views they show, which achieves a more realistic 3D representation.

Producing an isometric drawing

The key difference between axonometric and isometric drawings is that the isometric is created from a plan that is redrawn at a 30-degree distortion (as opposed to the 45-degree tilt of a redrawn axonometric plan). Once the plan is redrawn at this angle, an isometric drawing is produced in exactly the same way as an axonometric one (all lines are projected vertically to produce a 3D rendering of the object).

Isometric drawings are not quick to produce; time needs to be taken to draw the plan at the distorted and tricky angle of 30 degrees before the 3D view can be achieved. Certain elements, particularly circular shapes, are very difficult to draw in an isometric form.

Isometric drawings can become cutaway or exploded representations to exaggerate aspects of a concept or idea. Variations in color, texture, and shade can also be used to make the image appear more effective.

The advantage with both isometric and axonometric drawings is that they realistically connect with our natural sense of perception; they are more immediate interpretations of a building or space. They can be used equally well to describe concepts, buildings or details, and they effectively incorporate aspects of exterior, interior, elevation, and form in one representation.

4.10

Project: Conceptual
Location: Atlas Mountains, Morocco
Designer: Paul Cashin

These isometric drawings provide an exploded view of a scheme for living in the Atlas Mountains. Each drawing is created on the same framework and has been overlaid with explanations of zoning, massing water and ventilation strategies.

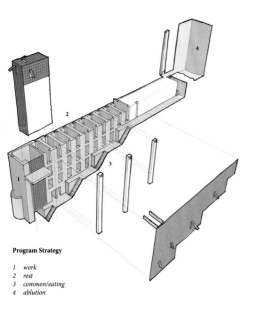

Program Strategy

1   *work*
2   *rest*
3   *common/eating*
4   *ablution*

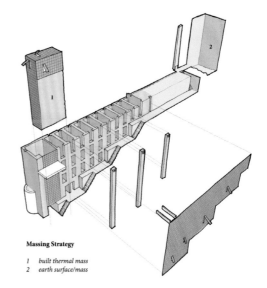

Massing Strategy

1   *built thermal mass*
2   *earth surface/mass*

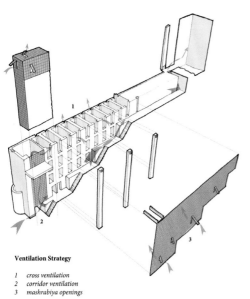

Ventilation Strategy

1   *cross ventilation*
2   *corridor ventilation*
3   *mashrabiya openings*

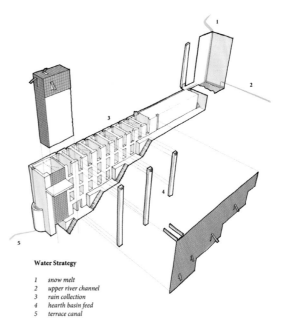

Water Strategy

1   *snow melt*
2   *upper river channel*
3   *rain collection*
4   *hearth basin feed*
5   *terrace canal*

4.10

Other applications

3D images can be used both to concentrate the viewer's eye of a particular aspect of a design, or to describe or deconstruct concepts and ideas. There is an essence of both realism and imagined possibilities about these images, and as such, they provide an accessible way to better understand a building. In addition to perspective, axonometric and isometric drawings, other forms of 3D representation are also available to the architect.

Fly-through views

Fly-through views are usually produced in a series and are generated from a 3D CAD model. Each image in the series is joined together using editing software to create a film that simulates the viewer "flying" through the architectural scheme. Fly-through presentations can create an impressive means to view a scheme and understand all its 3D spaces.

Wire frame models and images

Wireframe models provide a means to view a building in CAD software. These models only display the outline of the building, but they can still be a useful tool for understanding the building in its early development stages and how it might further develop as a 3D form. A wireframe image is essentially a transparent image, which allows the viewer to see the building as a 3D outline.

Interior views

3D interior views help describe an interior concept or space. These views can be enhanced to show furniture and fitting details, suggest the proposed materials and color schemes, and incorporate figures to provide a sense of scale. These drawings can also suggest the activities and functions that the design supports.

Sectional perspective

Sectional perspectives are a composite representation of section and perspective drawings. They can reveal connections within the design scheme as well as how different areas are intended to work together. In these drawings, the descriptions of the suggested activities and the view of space in the perspective are extremely important.

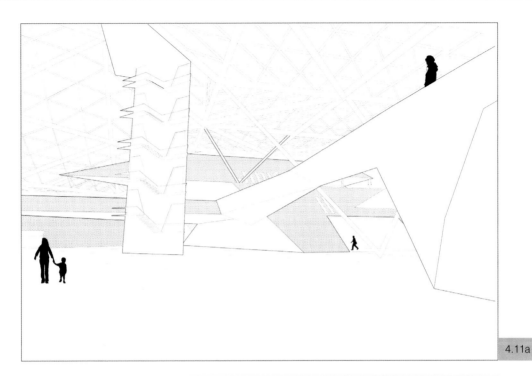

4.11a

4.11a–4.11b

Project: Libyan Heritage Museum
Location: Tripoli, Libya
Designer: Metropolitan Workshop

This computer-generated wireframe drawing and visualization is of a museum. The building concept is inspired by the tented desert structures used by the Bedouin and by the sand dunes in the Libyan landscape. The large, perforated canopy houses three exhibition pavilions beneath. The impact of being beneath the origami-like roof canopy is captured in the wireframe view of the interior.

4.11b

Cut-away drawings

Cut-away drawings reveal the inside of a building or shape, which means they can be an effective way to explore the relationship between the outside and the inside of a building, or to explain the structure or construction of a building and how it relates to the original concept or idea. These drawings are often isometric or axonometric and are presented as a model with a plane, wall, or section removed to give visual access to the inside of a building or shape.

Collage images

Images can be created that are a mixture of real photographs of places or models with layering of computer visualized drawings to produce a unique 3D effect.

VISUALISATIONS

WALKWAY FROM NORTH LAINES

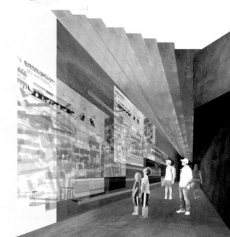

DIGITAL GALLERY SPACE

4.12

Project: Design Center
Location: Brighton, UK
Designer: Aivita Mateika

These computer-generated images have been enhanced with the application of collage. This gives the view a sense of reality. The inclusion of people and furniture gives a sense of scale.

4.12

NIGHT TIME VIEW

Presentation drawings

Presentation drawings can employ the best means of 3D representation to focus on a particular aspect of the architectural idea. Presentation drawings can be produced for a client, the public, or for a user group, so they need to communicate the concept with direct relevance to their intended audience and outline the benefits of the architecture for their needs and requirements.

Spatial sequences

A series of 3D drawings can orchestrate a sense of looking around or through an image. Spatial sequences can be used to explain an important aspect of the design concept such as a route through the building or the means of access and entry to it.

4.13

Project: Clone House
Location: Conceptual
Architect: CJ Lim/Studio 8 Architects

This series of 3D images describe a variety of permutations for CJ Lim's Clone House layout. The layout is a series of four rooms that can be configured in a variety of arrangements. The 3D images, alongside associated plan diagrams, explain these arrangements.

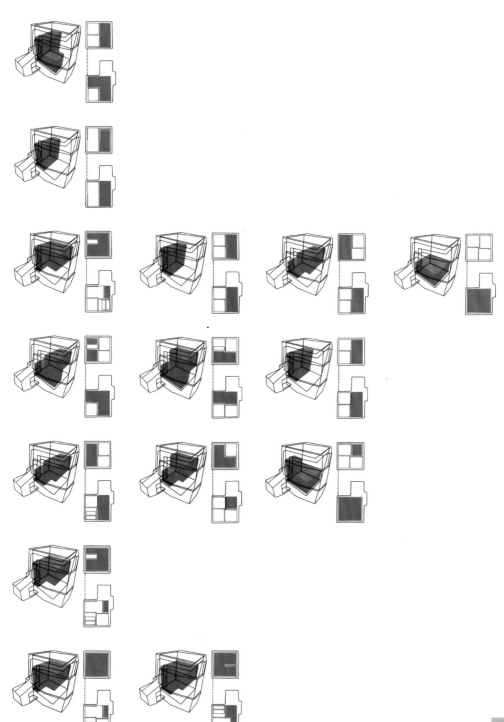

4.13

Photomontage and collage

One of the easiest ways to create a sense of reality with an architectural idea is to create a photomontage. This technique produces a composite image by cutting, joining, and layering a number of other photographs. In terms of architectural representation, a photomontage image takes an existing view and superimposes onto it a view of a scheme, building, or design. A photomontage could be a perspective view or a view of the scheme's plans or elevations.

The photomontage technique can be so seamless that the viewer can "believe" the proposed idea. The power of photomontage is that it combines actual photographs or impressions of places with imagined ideas of architecture, and the resultant image looks "real". Photomontage images are an important means to convince the viewer that the architecture can respond to its site or context effectively.

Traditionally, architectural photomontages were created by photographing a site and a physical model of a proposed scheme. These two photographs were then layered on top of one another (the photograph of the model would overlay that of the site), which produced a realistic impression of the scheme. Now, with software programs such as Photoshop, a digital image of the site can have an image of a CAD model or physical model superimposed on it to create an impression of the final scheme.

Collage

Collage derives from the French word *coller* (to stick). This technique produces a composite image by arranging, layering, and sticking various materials (such as photographs or fabric swatches) to a backing. Artists, such as George Braque (1882–1963) and Pablo Picasso (1881–1973), used collage to juxtapose images and objects in order to create abstract works of art.

Architects use collage to create a layered image. These layers may be visual fragments of proposed or existing sites, buildings or objects, and may include a plan, perspective and digital images, and 2- and 3D drawings in the same composite visual. Collage offers a much more abstract representation of an idea than photomontage. Collage is often more suggestive of a reality; architects using collage to represent their ideas do not intend to show a photorealistic impression.

4.14

Project: Pig Tower
Location: London, UK
Architect: CJ Lim/Studio 8
Architects

The Pig Tower is a conceptual project located in Smithfield's meat market. The scheme is inspired by the children's fairy tale 'The Three Little Pigs' and is a design for three towers.

This collage drawing is inspired by the restaurant within one of the towers and is created around a place setting (with cutlery).

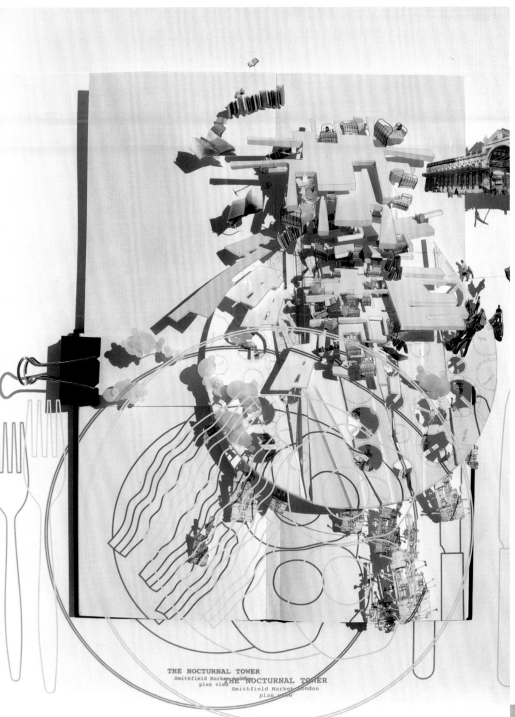

THE NOCTURNAL TOWER
Smithfield Market London
plan view

THE NOCTURNAL TOWER
Smithfield Market London
plan view

4.14

Case study: The Celestial River, UK by CJ Lim/Studio 8 Architects

"The Celestial River" is a conceptual proposal for a new transport system for London, UK. It seeks to reconfigure London Underground's Circle Line by lifting the tracks above the ground towards the sky (celestial) in order to create a continuous flow of transport above London, like a river. The "sky-river" suggests a solution to traffic congestion by offering an alternative method of transport. The scheme is part of a collection of visions commissioned by the BBC (British Broadcasting Corporation) based on concepts of place inspired by stories such as Lewis Carroll's *Alice in Wonderland* and Charles Dickens' *A Tale of Two Cities*. The visions are conceptual and will not be realized.

Unlike traditional architectural drawings, this collage drawing is conceptual. Drawings, photographs, models, and texts are all different expressions of ideas that can be used independently and collectively to represent architecture as a physical building.

The representation of "The Celestial River" is a combination of collage, drawing, and model-making techniques assembled together. The paper's surface is cut, folded, and transformed into three dimensions giving the drawing depth and shadow. It is layered with collaged images to provide narrative and a sense of scale. For example, the dragon boats represent movement, the clouds indicate sky, and the people show activity; from these representations, viewers can create their own stories. The cut layer of paper is woven with yarns to give the structure of the transport routes— a combination of reality and fantasy.

The image requires interpretation, as it can appear "real". Does the building or space actually exist or is it an impression of the building on a site or in a street? The use of collage challenges our sense of reality by inspiring imagination and curiosity.

The purpose of the project was to demonstrate that architectural representation is not just a flat picture of a future building. Drawings and models have a direct influence on the way a project develops as an idea or concept, and how the form of a building is generated. Images can transform our understanding of a concept and allow for multiple interpretations of an idea.

4.15

**Project: The Celestial River
Location: London, UK
Architect: CJ Lim/Studio 8 Architects**

The concept behind this collage is of a 3D experience. This vision uses pictures of dragon boats and people; it projects space and time and indicates movement. Each element is layered against the next with the surface of paper being cut to give further depth.

4.15

"At every instant there is more than the eye can see, more than the ear can
hear, a setting or a view waiting to be explored."
Kevin Leach from *The Image of a City*

Project: Serial and perspective views

Perspective views can be used in a sequence to illustrate a journey through a design proposal. This sequence is called a "serial vision" as it describes a journey through a city. Each view connects to the next to provide an impression of the journey seen from a single point.

This scheme is for an Argan oil-processing and bottling center in the village of Setti Fatima in the Ourika Valley, Morocco. The concept is for the arrival through the landscape. The sequence of perspectives illustrates this journey. Each perspective view explores a key view of the overall sequence and defines particular vistas and connections through the designed spaces.

Process

This step-by-step guide teaches how to set up a single-point perspective so that a sequence of serial views can be created.

1 Plan your sequence

- Use a site or building plan and plan a route through your scheme.

- Consider how each image links to the next and establish points of focus.

2 Set up your perspective sketch

- On tracing paper, draw a horizontal line in pencil. This is the horizon line and represents the eye height of the viewer.

- Mark the vanishing point on this horizon line. All lines will converge into the vanishing point.

- Draw the forward face or edge of the object. This could be the frame, elevation, or surface, which will act as the picture plane (image plane).

- Draw in pencil, perspective lines from the vanishing point through the edges of your object (picture plane).

- Draw the verticals and horizontals between the perspective lines. Within single-point perspective, vertical lines remain vertical and parallel lines remain parallel.

- Fill in the detail of the perspective drawing. Trace over the construction lines and add line weights. Drawing shadows and blocking in surfaces helps to emphasize detail.

- Add a figure to give a sense of scale to the perspective. Eyeline is always on the horizon line.

- Figures should get smaller as they move towards the center of the image and towards the vanishing point.

4.16a–4.16d

Project: Center for the processing of Argan oil
Location: Setti Fatima, Morocco
Designer: Darren Leach

This sequence of images illustrates how to draw a single point perspective with the construction of a viewpoint, horizon line, standpoint, and picture plane.

Image 4.16a uses hand- and computer-drawing techniques. The colored surfaces indicating the ground and sky extend beyond the drawing to give it a further sense of depth.

4.16a

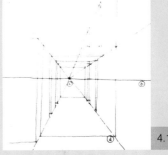

4.16b

4.16c

4.16d

Practice using perspective

- SketchUp software can assist in creating quick framework drawings that can be overdrawn by hand.

- Add collaged textures, tone, and people to the perspectives with Photoshop.

- Test the horizon line and vanishing point to manipulate the views. Moving the horizon line up defines if you are looking up or down.

- Extend the guidelines beyond the perspective drawing and emphasis will be given to the perspective and sense of depth.

- Emphasize the connection between the views with accents of color.

5.1

5 Modeling

Modeling allows an architect to explore an idea in a 3D form. Models communicate an architectural idea in an accessible way, immediately showing aspects of scale, form, and material. A model can be produced as a full-size prototype of an element (such as a door or window) at the scale of a room, or at the scale of a city (in the form of an urban model). Physical models allow an idea to be explored in greater depth as certain elements of the scheme or their scale may not be understood until they are seen in the context of a model form.

CAD visualizations offer impressively realistic models that allow the viewer to choose how they move through a building. CAD models can be used to develop complex forms in the design process, allowing shapes to evolve and explore a range of forms.

5.1

Project: Proposal to regenerate the Agrigento, Sicily
Location: Agrigento, Italy
Designers: Dean Fitton and Graham Lake

Using a CAD model on a laser cutting created this model's professional appearance. The CAD model allowed a section of the scheme to be shown with a high degree of accuracy in the laser cutting of woods and acrylics. Layered acrylic has been used to represent the existing building and timber for the new inserted decks. Prior to the final model, a series of card models made by hand were used to test ideas.

Physical models

Physical models were a popular device in the Renaissance period (during the fifteenth and early sixteenth centuries in different regions of Europe), and they were often relied upon as the sole means of describing an architectural idea. Drawings became the main method for architectural expression during the Beaux-Arts period (during the late nineteenth and early twentieth centuries), but from the mid-1900s, architects once again began to see the benefits of physical models as a means to communicate and shape their ideas.

Even in today's digital world, with the advances of CAD technologies, the physical model still has an important place. It has a texture and physical presence that can be interrogated and understood. It can be viewed from many directions and suggests materiality and form.

A physical model can be made at any stage of the architectural design process, from initial concept right up to the presentation of the finished scheme. However, different types of physical models tend to be used at different stages of the design process. Whatever the type, critical considerations when producing a physical model are scale, materials, and the model's relationship to the design concept.

Concept models

A concept model will describe an idea in simple terms in order to clearly communicate the underlying architectural concept. It may be that the choice of material or use of color is crucial for this type of model in order to isolate and exaggerate the idea, and ensure it is clearly and correctly understood. At this stage of the design process, models that explore volume (massing) are used, which explore architectural form. These are a useful type of concept model as they can be quickly built to scale using materials such as foam, wood, or card, and they provide an understanding of the relationship between the different site areas.

Curved forms are challenging to model. The following process was followed: an initial solid egg-shaped core was made from foam (solid) and fiberglass (shell), which would be finally clad with cedar veneer strips to reflect the actual finish of the egg. The scale drawings were used at all stages in order to create accurate molds and details during the final cladding of the exterior.

5.2

5.2
___

**Project: Model of Exbury Egg
Location: Exbury Gardens,
Southampton, UK
Designer: Matt Sedgewick,
based on a design by PAD
Studio**

This storyboard illustrates
making the shell of the Exbury
Egg, a floating artist's studio
formed using a timber structure
within Exbury Gardens.

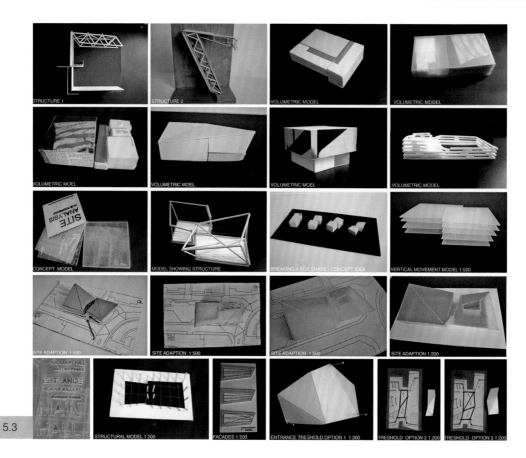

5.3

5.3

Project: Sports hall proposal
Location: Brighton, UK
Designer: Aivita Mateika

This sectional model explores
the design for a sports hall
within a tight urban site. The
section model reveals the
interior quality of the space
and uses layers of MDF, foam
board, veneer, and acetate.
This model is supported with a
series of models that explore
the building's exterior form; they
can be tested when inserted
into the site model.

FINAL MODEL 1:200

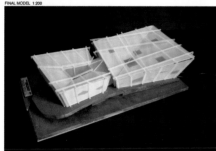

GROUP MODEL 1:200

Development models

Development models are produced at various stages of the design process and are intended to align the scheme's concept with the brief's specifications. These models can inform stages of the design process and may change radically as the scheme progresses. They offer the quickest means for solving and exploring 3D problems, and exploiting the potential for design development (as the viewer can look over, through, inside, and outside a development model). A development model can be used equally well as a basis for discussion between the client and the design team, or as a means for testing a particular aspect of the scheme.

Illuminated models

Illuminated models can create an impressive effect by incorporating miniature bulbs, fiber optics, transparent, or semi-opaque materials. These models are often used to highlight particular aspects of a scheme or design.

As well as creating an impressive aesthetic, illuminated models can lend themselves well to representing certain projects. For example, buildings that are used heavily in the evening (such as theaters, restaurants, or bars) will have a different physical presence at night than they do in the day, and an illuminated model can suggest the impact that the lit building will have on its immediate environment.

Presentation models

These are models of the final scheme. They may be used for the purposes of public consultation before a scheme starts or they may provide an overview of the finished building for a client.

The scale of the presentation model, and the volume of surrounding architecture or landscape that it displays, needs to be carefully considered. If, for example, a project relates to particular reference points in the surrounding area, such as an important building, road, or route, then these should be included in the model as they will affect the design development.

Physical modeling equipment

Contrary to what you may think, you don't require complicated specialist tools or materials to make physical models. Professional model-makers may use sophisticated machinery to obtain impressive and highly accurate finished models, but most architects use slightly more rudimentary tools to construct their own models.

Through model-making at full size, real design challenges can be explored. The full-size models are accompanied by timber conceptual models, which test how the buildings are inserted into the ground.

5.4

Project: Prototyping
Location: Ourika Valley, Morocco
Designers: Toby Richardson and Sam Sclater-Brooks

This series of images illustrates a range of full-size model-making techniques. The model is of a rammed earth wall, which has been made within timber formwork. A formwork is a temporary mold in which materials are poured.

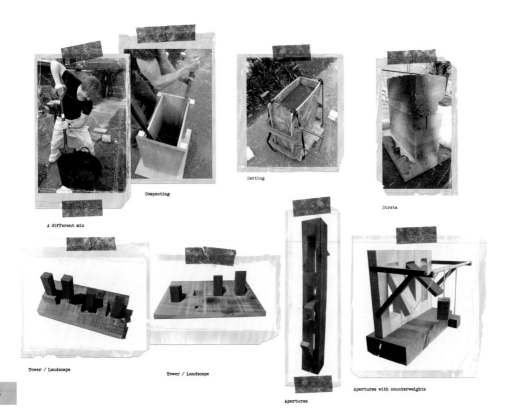

A different mix

Compacting

Setting

Strata

Tower / Landscape

Tower / Landscape

Apertures

Apertures with counterweights

Tools

To make models, the basic tools required are a cutting mat, a metal ruler, scissors, knives, and hot-wire cutters.

A cutting mat provides a base on which to cut materials. This is normally made of rubber, but a piece of hard board or other tough surface can also be used. Rubber cutting mats have a grid printed onto them to allow straight lines to be cut quickly and easily.

Metal rules provide a clear edge to cut against and will prevent the knife from slicing into the rule when in use (an advantage that a plastic rule won't have). Never use a scale rule to cut against because the knife will score its edge.

Sharp knives are important for cutting materials cleanly and precisely. The cut of the material is important, so take time and make your incisions carefully. If a material is cut at an angle, it won't look like a clean edge when it is joined with another piece.

A scalpel blade is the most useful knife as it will be extremely sharp. It needs to be used with extreme care as too much pressure will cause the blade to snap. Any knife work needs to be done in good light, cutting slowly and carefully.

Scissors can only be used for cutting paper and very thin card. If using wood as a modeling material, then tools such as a bench saw, table saw, or jigsaw are necessary for accurate cutting.

Hot-wire cutters slice through foam accurately and leave a clean edge. Their fine wire is heated electrically, and the wire's malleable quality allows shapes drawn onto the foam to be cut quickly by pushing the material against the wire. This is a fast way to make a model of a city; a map of the area can be drawn onto the foam, which is then cut to produce block shapes.

Materials

The choice of material used to construct any model will relate to the speed with which the model needs to be made, the stage of the design idea, and what the model is aiming to explore or explain. To decide which materials to incorporate in your model, it is necessary to consider whether it needs to be representative of the "real" materials that are to be used in the design scheme, or whether you want to produce a "neutral" model, which concentrates on the building form and mass.

"Real" models can represent a material quality of the architectural idea. In some cases, the model could be made of a similar material to that intended for the finished building; however, this is not always appropriate or practical.

Sometimes it may only be necessary to demonstrate a particular characteristic of the building's material in the model form. For example, if an architectural design incorporates a metal roof that is intended to be highly reflective, this could be emphasized by using metal, while other materials may be representative of the building's form.

Neutral models

Models that are made of materials such as card or wood can be described as neutral. The final scheme will almost always be made of other materials, but neutral materials will sufficiently represent the mass and form of the scheme on its site.

When choosing the material for your model, it can be a good idea to consider any surrounding buildings on the site. Proposed and existing scheme models will read more clearly if each is differentiated by material type or color. Also, the scale of the model will have an impact on the materials it is to be built from. A model showing a city will have less detail than one showing an interior, and more detailed models may have layers of material applied to them to create interest or a sense of realism.

Card

Card is available in many weights and colors and can be cut accurately with a knife to achieve a straight edge. These properties make it a versatile material for model-making. Corrugated card can be self-supporting, which makes it a good material for a model's walls or roof. Also, the corrugated edge can be used to suggest particular finishes on the building.

Foam board

Foam board describes a piece of foam that is sandwiched between two thin pieces of card. It is available in a variety of weights, which means that it is a useful material for representing different wall widths. It is also a fairly sturdy material, so it is self-supporting on smaller models. Colored foam board can be used to suggest different material finishes.

Polystyrene and styrofoam

Polystyrene is very flexible and can be cut and shaped easily to create organic forms. Styrofoam is a board material that can be easily cut, shaped, glued, and painted. It has a finely textured surface that provides a smooth finish for model-making. It is also lightweight, easy to handle, and reusable.

Wood

Models made from wood can be easily adapted and developed. Most commonly used for model-making, balsa wood comes from a tropical tree source and is very light (it has a density that is a third of other hardwoods), so it is easy to cut, which is good for creating accurate models.

Other woods can be used to provide particular finishes. Cork, for example, can be used to give a carpet-like effect to a surface, which is useful for city-scale models.

Wood can be finely sanded and varnished to achieve a range of finishes, and using different woods in varying grains or colors will affect the appearance of your model.

5.5a

5.5a–5.5b

Project: Conceptual model
Location: Hilsea Lido,
Portsmouth, UK
Designer: Ricardo Marques

This concept model (image
5.5a) illustrates a ribbed
structure and is made from
recycled card. Each of the card
ribs is mounted on a baseboard
with a contrasting floor deck
applied on top.

The lighting of a model is
important. Image 5.5b uses
artificial light as its source to
create shadows that give an
added sense of depth to the
image. When using an artificial
light source, ensure you
consider the orientation of
your scheme.

5.5b

5.6

5.6

Project: Competition Model,
World Trade Center
Location: New York, USA
Architect: Studio Daniel
Libeskind

Daniel Libeskind's design for
the World Trade Center
Master Plan in New York uses
contrasting model-making
materials to represent the
proposed towers. The model
is made from Perspex, which
is a transparent material that
allows the structural shapes
to be read through the
building frame. The existing
buildings are constructed
from timber to contrast with
the transparent towers.

Metal

In model-making, metal can be used in
sheet form to suggest various building
finishes, wall cladding, or roofing. The
sheets can be made from aluminum,
copper, brass, or steel and can be
perforated or corrugated, or in mesh or
flat-sheet form.

Transparent materials

These can lend interesting qualities to a
physical model. Perspex and acrylic can
be completely transparent or have a
semi-opaque finish, and colored
acrylics can be used to good effect in
model-making. Using lights to illuminate
transparent material will exaggerate the
effect of the design's features.

Color

Color can be used within a monochromatic model to reveal surface and/or texture and bring focus to it. Depending on the ideas being communicated, contrast of either material or color can be effective. Color, or the lack thereof, may bring articulation and a shift in the hierarchy reading of a model or model elements.

Scale and finishes

Introducing objects for which we understand the scale will make a model appear more realistic and help the viewer to understand the proportions of the architecture. These objects might be model figures, cars, or trees—any elements that are immediately accessible to the viewer.

The finish should be an important consideration at all stages of the model's construction. Time needs to be taken when cutting materials to ensure that they are cut accurately, and care must be taken when assembling the pieces. This care will ensure that the model is considered as an important part of the whole design presentation.

Notes on adhesives

Different materials will require different adhesives to allow them to fix properly. Always ensure that the appropriate glues are used; if not, the model will not stick together or the glue may mark or even dissolve the material of the model.

- Some adhesives will dry to a transparent finish, which may be important.

- Adhesive spray allows pieces to be stuck together and then repositioned. This is useful for fixing paper and thin card.

- PVA (polyvinyl acetate) glue is general-purpose glue that is good for porous materials such as wood.

- Glue dots can be placed on pieces of material that are then pushed together to produce a clean finish.

- Contact adhesives, as the name suggests, affix materials on contact.

- Specialist glues are needed for certain materials. Balsa cement, for example, is good for balsa and other lightweight woods.

- Tape is a useful tool for holding glued pieces together while they fix. Masking tape won't leave marks on the modeling materials and double-sided tape allows two materials to fix together quickly.

- Glue guns give a quick, fast-drying effect.

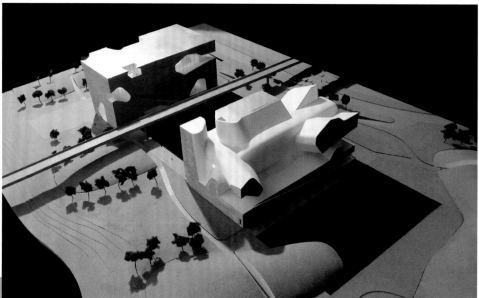

5.7a

Model scales

Although some physical models take an abstract form and so are not to scale (similarly, initial architectural models, such as concept models, explore ideas of material and form, and these models may not use scale), the use of scale can offer an advantage in model-making as it allows an appreciation of the real or perceived size of a proposed building or space.

As an architectural idea develops the scale at which it is investigated changes (refer to page 37):

- An urban model showing the master plan of a city will be produced at 1:2500 or 1:1250 scale. This is roughly the same scale as a map and allows aspects of the city to be read in connection with one another.

- A model of a large building will relate to its site at 1:500 scale and as the idea develops, the scale of investigation changes until it becomes a model at 1:50 or 1:20 scale, which is approximately the size of a standard room.

- Models produced at 1:10, 1:5 or 1:2 scale are normally used to describe the material details of a building or space, or how its component parts will join and fit together.

- Some physical models are made at actual or real size. If a building component (for example a window, frame, or roof) has to be specially tested, then it may be manufactured and reproduced as a full-size prototype. Real-size models allow close examination of the proposed building component in its true form.

Photographing models

Although a model may well be intended to be viewed and investigated in 3D form, if it is photographed, then it can also be included in a portfolio of work, or in the creation of CAD images or photomontage and collage images. Important considerations when photographing models are:

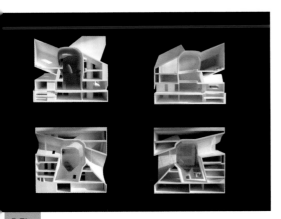

5.7b

5.7a–5.7b

Project: Tianjin EcoCity Ecology and Planning Museums
Location: Tianjin, China
Architect: Steven Holl Architects

Models are very effective means of exploring the sectional idea of a building. They can be photographed to create a series of views (as shown here). The sectional model describes how the building volume is carved and how various floor levels work within the scheme.

- Stage the views and use a neutral background, such as a white or black sheet, that will contrast with the model.

- If possible, try and photograph your model outdoors using the sky as a backdrop. This can add to the overall realism of the piece.

- Consider light and shadow falling on the model. Orient it as it should be in reality, and this will make the model a truer representation of the scheme.

- Ensure that there aren't any objects or elements in the frame of the photograph that will affect the scale illusion of the model.

- Photograph the model from all angles as overview images and then zoom in to capture details. This will provide a range of views of the model for use in other presentations.

- In some cases, it can be useful to photograph the different stages of the model's construction as this will show the stages of development of the idea.

CAD models

CAD assists the generation of 2D plan, section, and elevation drawings as well as the creation of 3D interactive models.

Originally developed in the 1960s for commercial application in the aerospace and electronic industries, CAD was further developed for desktop computer use during the 1980s. Autodesk and AutoCAD were the first CAD software programs developed for PCs (1981). Macintosh-based systems were developed and made available later in the decade. Today, most CAD software programs work across both platforms.

Generally, CAD schemes are "drawn" on screen using a mouse, but some systems use a pen and graphics tablet. In such systems, the CAD software renders lines and points made by the stylus onto the computer screen.

Creating CAD models offers the architect the possibility to show the scheme at any stage during its development, to quickly adapt a design and respond to changes in the project brief, and to show impressive graphics and a range of interior and exterior views of a building or space.

Rapid prototyping

Rapid prototyping refers to a modeling process that can fabricate a physical scale model using 3D CAD data. What is commonly considered to be the first rapid prototyping technique, stereolithography, was developed in 1986 by 3D Systems, based in Valencia, CA, USA.

Rapid prototyping is also referred to as "solid free-form manufacturing", "computer-automated manufacturing", and "layered manufacturing". All four labels essentially refer to the same workflow; a computer is connected to machinery that interprets the data and creates the 3D model. The model is then produced by the machine using layers of paper, plastic, or other materials. Rapid prototyping means that the exact same model exists in both virtual (CAD) and physical form.

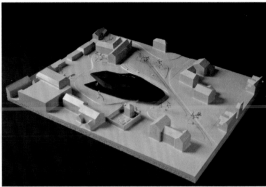

5.8

5.8

Project: Conceptual 3D printed model
Location: Portsmouth, UK
Designer: Nora Pucher and Christoph Zechmeister

This model has been printed from the data held within a CAD model that allows complicated organic forms to be modeled physically and digitally. In this example, a city model has been created from dense foam, which has been milled on a CNC (computer numerical control) machine and the building printed in 3D. The same CAD model has been used to create these models.

CAD software

To make a CAD model effectively, it is useful to have access to a range of different pieces of software. CAD software can be broadly categorized as programs that offer the functionality to create 2D drawings, 3D models, and hybrids that produce both.

When using CAD software, it is important to experiment with different applications as each will have varying advantages, from sophisticated film and editing possibilities to rendering packages that produce realistic impressions of any building material. Most drawing packages are constantly updated and reissued as new versions of the program offer improved tools and associated facilities. Over the last few years, advances in CAD software functionality have created the possibility for impressively realistic models.

CAD at different stages of the design process

The production of CAD drawings and models should not be considered as a replacement for the creation of physical models, freehand drawings, or sketches. Instead, CAD software can facilitate the development of shapes and forms that could not be created via plan, section, and elevation drawings. As such, it is a tool to be used at critical points during the design process.

The first of these points is at the initial massing stage of a project. CAD models can be used here to create an overall impression of the scale of a proposed building, and suggest its outline form as well as its likely impact on the surrounding context.

A second key advantage is that interior CAD models can show a "fly-through" series of images (see page 149), moving the viewer through a "film" of the proposed scheme. Many CAD software programs offer the functionality to both direct and edit a fly-through sequence of views from a model.

Finally, using CAD rendering packages means that material finishes can be scanned and applied (just like wallpaper) onto the models. These packages can also offer lighting options, projecting shadow inside and around a building, which can create an even greater sense of realism.

5.9

Project: Oxford Bookes University Campus
Location: Oxford, UK
Architect: Design Engine

This CAD image shows the interior volumes within the scheme. It uses a monochrome palette with accents of color to identify key navigation points, for example the circulation core and corridor walls.

5.9

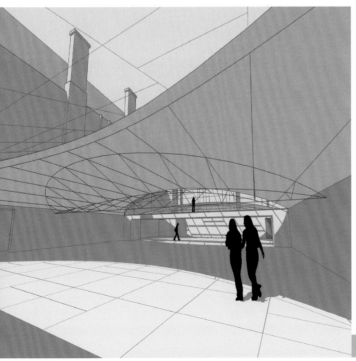

5.10

5.10

**Project: Oxford University
examination hall
Location: Oxford, UK
Architect: Design Engine**

Models can be used to describe
concepts in a variety of ways.
Here, Design Engine architects
use a wireframe model to create
a transparent frame from which
to generate views of the space
of the examination hall in
Oxford University.

Ideas to CAD

As well as allowing impressive visuals, CAD software has afforded a new type of architecture. Complex forms, which were not previously possible, can now be modeled in CAD programs and their form, structure, and materials tested. CAD technology is critical for these sort of architectural forms; quite simply, physical models cannot fully explore such ideas sufficiently enough to convince the client and engineers of the possibility of the design.

Specific CAD applications are used for modeling these new architectural forms. Vectorworks is a drawing package that is very useful for creating 2D plan, section, and elevation drawings. It also offers a 3D modeling package.

ArchiCAD originated as a 3D modeling package, but it now has the functionality to produce 2D drawings as well. It can be used with additional software to create realistic material finishes and fly-through views of the scheme.

AutoCAD is universally available and is used by many architects and engineers as their standard drawing software.

Google SketchUp can be used to build and modify 3D models quickly and easily. If used in conjunction with Google Earth, SketchUp allows you to place your models on-site using actual coordinates and share them via Google 3D Warehouse.

Rendering packages, such as Artlantis or Autodesk 3D Studio Max, work with other drawing programs to create impressive material and color finishes to models.

5.11a

5.11a–5.11c

Project: The Visitor Centre, Hardwick Park
Location: Durham, UK
Architect: Design Engine

These CAD images form part of a proposal for a new visitor center. The center's form is designed using "bridge-building" technology; each skeletal sector is clad in corten steel for a naturally protected "rust" finish. It sits as a found object within the woodland site.

5.11b

5.11c

Google SketchUp and Google Earth

Google SketchUp is available to download from www.sketchup.com. It is an easy-to-use and intuitive piece of software that allows 3D shapes to be formed quickly. Once the form has been created, SketchUp has the functionality to allow apertures to be created in the shape to suggest doors and windows.

Google Earth software allows any location in the world to be viewed as an aerial photograph or street view, though some areas display more detail than others. Google Earth can be used in conjunction with SketchUp, which means that you can draw a form in SketchUp and place that form on a location image generated in Google Earth. This allows you to create images that not only show a structural concept but also allow them to be viewed in a realistic context.

A number of extension programs are now available that allows you to manipulate the model—for example, add texture or prepare the model to print to 3D (extensions.sketchup.com).

CAD to digital modeling

A CAD drawing can be used to create a physical model. This model can be created using a variety of different pieces of hardware: 3D printers, which convert the CAD image into a 3D object; and computer-numeric controlled (CNC) machinery that cuts through various materials to form a physical model. There are laser-cut models that cut large sheets or boards into plans or other 2D forms. These new technologies are enabling a range of various outputs.

Drawing file formats

Many software programs support the transfer of data and drawings between one platform and another. If the drawings are saved as neutral file types, then they can be accessed across programs.

- DWG files originated in the AutoCAD software package but have since become the standard file type to exchange drawing files. The DXF file format is a variant. Most CAD programs (such as AutoCAD, Autodesk, MicroStation, Vectorworks and ArchiCAD) use the DWG format.

- Drawings can also be saved as JPEG files and transferred from one piece of software to another. JPEG stands for "Joint Photographic Experts Group", which is the name of the committee that created the standard.

- STL is a file format native to stereolithography CAD software.

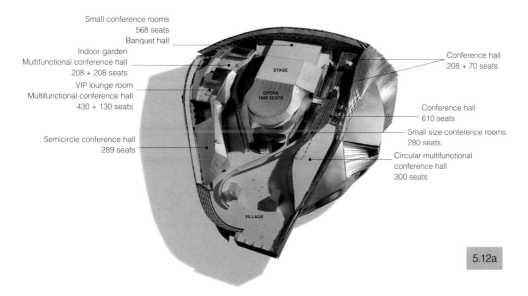

Small conference rooms
568 seats
Banquet hall
Indoor garden
Multifunctional conference hall
208 + 208 seats
VIP lounge room
Multifunctional conference hall
430 + 130 seats

Semicircle conference hall
289 seats

Conference hall
208 + 70 seats

Conference hall
610 seats

Small size conference rooms
280 seats

Circular multifunctional
conference hall
300 seats

STAGE

OPERA
1668 SEATS

VILLAGE

5.12a

5.12a–5.12b

**Project: Dalian International
Conference Center
Location: Dalian, China
Architect: Coop Himmelb(l)au**

These images show a cutaway
computer model that allows
the interior arrangement
to be viewed from above.
The conference center is
organized around a classical
theater auditorium, as well as
for the flexible multipurpose
hall. Annotations explain the
functions within the model.

CAD modeling has been
used to explore the skin of
the conference center and its
layers. This exploded view from
the model allows information to
be revealed or hidden and it to
be viewed as a wire frame.

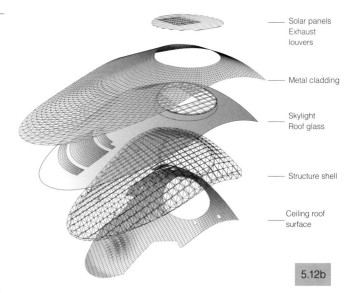

Solar panels
Exhaust
louvers

Metal cladding

Skylight
Roof glass

Structure shell

Ceiling roof
surface

5.12b

Building Information Modeling

Design teams use Building Information Modeling (BIM) to create 3D models of buildings. These models inform the design and construction of buildings. BIM uses a range of types of representations including CAD images, 3D modeling, and dynamic CAD models. The intention is that the entire building process is included, for example: structural design, lighting analysis, environmental systems, and building component details. A team of people contributes to this information system, which is constantly updated. It is used as a reference set of data and information for the building as a system.

Each user of the model whether an engineer, an architect, or a client, can draw information from this complex model to create more specific drawings, or isolate certain information, for example, a detail of part of a building, structural information, or plan layouts at various scales.

The model is used to work through any potential issues that might occur in coordinating design, such as the structural design, and mechanical and electrical design systems. The model is built in detail as a virtual environment; this is to enable examination of potential problem areas before construction begins on-site. It is also used in the construction phase of the project to inform the project management team should aspects of the project change.

5.13a–5.13c

**Project: BIM process model
Architect: RBA Architects**

This sequence of images illustrates the initial principles of creating a 3D Revit model. The model was part of a pilot program developed to demonstrate how BIM (Building Information Modeling) can be used as a collaborative tool.

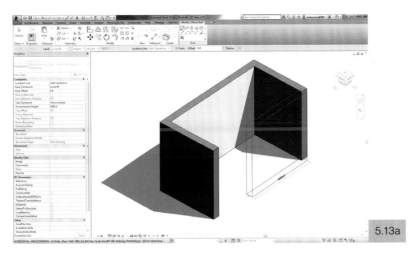

5.13a

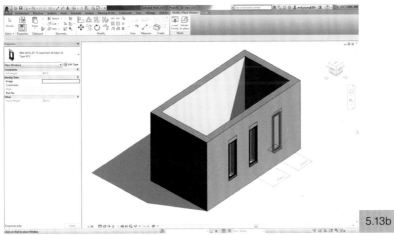

5.13b

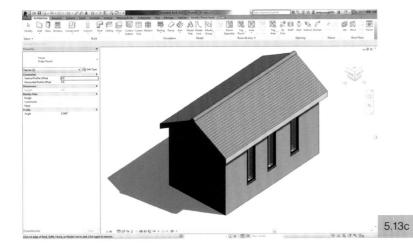

5.13c

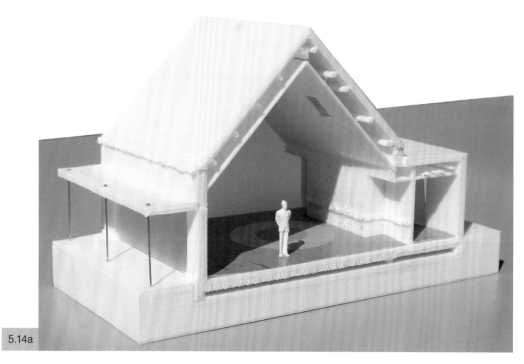

5.14a

Completion of building

When a system changes this is updated on the BIM model. If alterations are suggested, then the BIM model is used to provide all the drawing records of the building, saving time and money for the client.

Many types of software can be used in the BIM process. The important issue is that it is a software platform that can be used by all members of the construction team. Autodesk have BIM CAD software that they have developed as a shared software platform, which can be used to produce complex 3D and 2D models and drawings and also mechanical, electrical, and structural engineering design proposals.

5.14a–5.14c

Project: Classroom design
Location: Pilot project
Architect: Hampshire County Architects

These images are created from a shared BIM model and show a proposed classroom design. The model contains information provided by architects, consultants, and specialists.

The CAD model has been used to create a wireframe section image to show the services and structures. A physical model of the classroom has been printed in three dimensions from the collaborative CAD model to test the integration of the design.

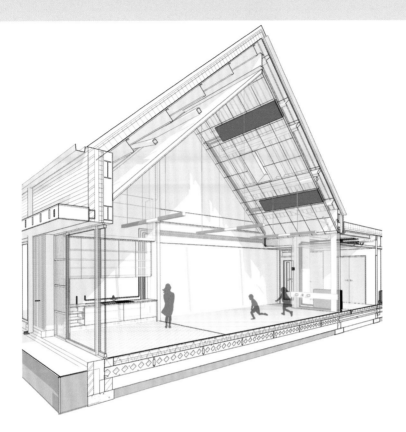

5.14b

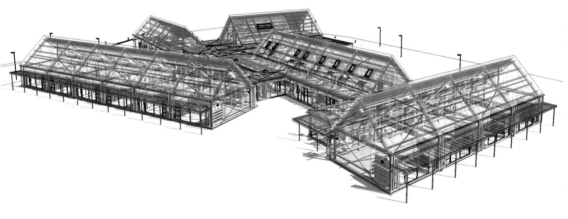

5.14c

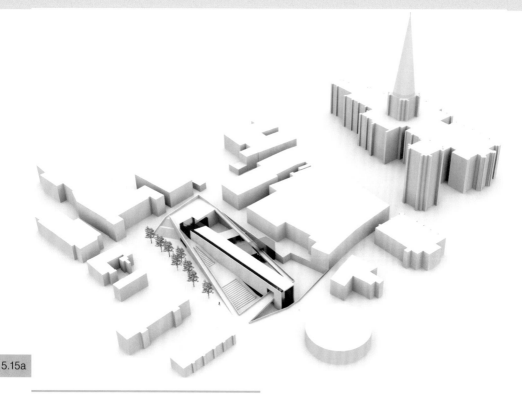

5.15a

Fly through

Whether a CAD or physical model is generated to represent, explain, and explore an architectural scheme, the advantage it has (over any drawn form) is that it allows many views of a building to be considered.

Many CAD software packages offer the facility to explore a 3D model using "fly-through" techniques. This technique describes the capturing of individual views from within the model and editing them to form a series of connected images that render as if one is "flying through" the building or space.

The fly-through technique can also be applied to a physical model by photographing it from a variety of angles and then assembling the images to suggest a journey through the proposed scheme that best describes the architectural concept.

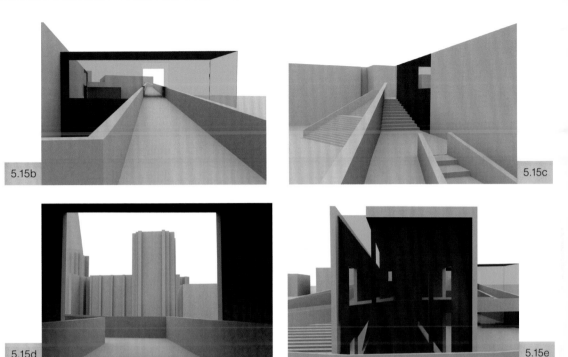

5.15b 5.15c 5.15d 5.15e

5.15a–5.15e

**Project: Chichester Museum
Location: Chichester, UK
Designer: Khalid Saleh**

These images show a sequential series of CAD models for a museum design. The museum's site is adjacent to an important cathedral precinct, and this location informed the concept for the proposal. The spire of the cathedral, for example, was visible at various points within the scheme.

The fly-through CAD images allow the journey through the scheme and the associated views to be understood. The images were created using a range of software. Initially, the scheme was drawn in Vectorworks software; it was then imported into SketchUp to create a 3D model and was finally rendered in Autodesk 3D Studio Max. The perspective images were edited in Photoshop.

Case study: Musée des Confluences, France by Coop Himmelb(l)au

From sketch to model

The Musée des Confluences is a new museum of science and society located on an island where the rivers Rhone and Saone converge, in Lyon, France. It has been designed by the Austrian practice Coop Himmelb(l)au. The central themes of the museum are concerned with technology, biology, and ethics, and the architecture needed to reflect these ideas. The resulting building is visually striking and has a complex sculptural form. The site is also part of an important landmark, which creates a new public space.

At the early stages of design, a building of this scale needs to be carefully modeled physically in three dimensions; this allows for the different shapes and forms to be explored and to examine their impact on the geography and topography of the site.

The museum consists of two connected architectural shapes: the "crystal" and the "cloud". The crystal is more open and glazed and houses the entrance hall for visitors; the cloud has a more dense form, and it is the exhibition space for the museum.

The site has created a new urban leisure area—a landscape consisting of ramps and surfaces. This idea connects the inside and the outside of the building and results in a dynamic sequence of spaces.

5.16a

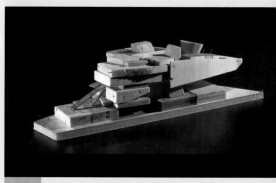

5.16b

The drawings for this scheme show the site location, which is on the edge of a park and at the point where the two rivers converge; the drawings reveal the relationship between inside and outside spaces. The flexible arrangement of the interior of the building and the exhibition spaces illustrate the adaptable nature of the building to accommodate new exhibitions. This scheme consists of a type of landscape as well as a built environment; both are described conceptually as well as through measured drawings.

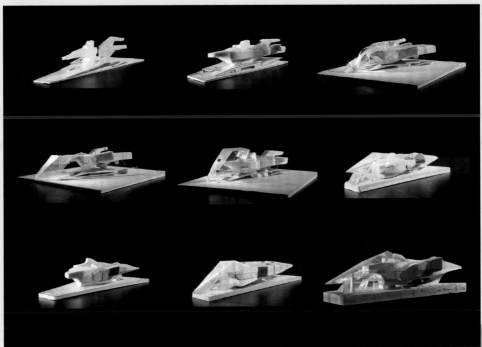

5.16c

5.16a–5.16c

Project: Musée des Confluences
Location: Lyon, France
Architects: Coop Himmelb(l)au

This architectural concept sketch (image 5.16a) reduces a series of complex ideas into only a few lines. It quickly maps the overall form, mass, and connection between elements. Although the sketch is not to scale, it can be understood due to the marks that represent figures.

Image 5.16b explores the program of the building at a larger scale. The model shows layers and volumes within the scheme.

Image 5.16c shows a sequence of massing models, which documents the working process of the design. Using a range of materials—foam board, card, trace, acetate, and low-density foam—the models explore form and composition.

Project: Hand to digital modeling

This student project explores different ways to make a model at the scale of the city using hand and digital techniques together in one model. The model does not aim to give a high degree of realism but instead demonstrate form, height, and texture of the city in a purposefully abstract way.

While hand modeling demonstrates a crafted quality, it can be time-consuming for repetitive elements. Digital fabrication produces repetitive elements quickly; it can include a high level of detail and reduce assembly time. This step-by-step guide introduces you to exploring digital fabrication together with hand model-making.

Process

1   Mark on a site plan (1:500 or 1:1250) the area you intend to model. Note the key landscape features and estimate building heights. Decide on the amount of hand and digital techniques.

2   Create a CAD model (to scale) containing your site information; this will be used in digital laser cutting and fabrication. If you are layering materials, you need to consider multiple elements.

3   Select materials suitable for laser cutting, for example: basswood, ply, vellum, paper, corrugated cardboard, or acrylic. Multiple layers can be cut and etched to communicate different levels of information.

4   Draw buildings, landscape, and roads on separate layers. Each layer will define how selected materials are cut or etched. Use colored lines to define the cut; for example, scoring shown in yellow, etching in blue, and cutting in magenta.

5   Follow the manufacturer's guidance to set up the cutting file. Allow time to create a test on the laser cutter. Adjust your files as needed. Cut when ready.

6   Once cut, name the elements clearly to ensure easy assembly. In images 5.17a–5.17d, buildings are made from acrylic and ply layered to create floors. These layers are fixed with contact adhesive.

7   Mark the road layout on card and cut with a scalpel. Overlay on a contrasting card to represent the landscape. Fix onto a wooden baseboard with PVA or spray glue.

8   Place the laser cut or handmade buildings onto the baseboard and fix with contact adhesive. Create a title block showing the project details, scale, and orientation.

Hints and tips

● Use gloves when handling easily marked materials to keep them clean.

● Laser cut a glue spreader out of the waste material.

● Over time, collect a store of materials suitable for model-making.

● Always mark the laser-cut pieces with sticky labels to remind you of the assembly order.

● Cutting on a laser cutter creates a vector line (DWG file type, for example), which is faster than cutting from an image such as a JPEG.

● Change the craft knife blade frequently.

5.17a

5.17a–5.17d

Project: City model
Location: Conceptual
Designers: Bruna Fleck and
Ioannis Miltiadou

These images of a city
model illustrate a variety of
model-making techniques
using both hand and digital
techniques. They show some
of the processes including
the use of laser cut materials
and acrylic.

5.17b

5.17c

5.17d

Hand modeling equipment
- Scale ruler (for measuring)
- Metal ruler
- Cutting mat
- Scalpel or craft knife with spare blades
- Contact adhesive and PVA glue
- A variety of model-making materials

48th- 54th FLOOR RESIDENTIAL
+ 871'-4 ½"- 936'-10 ¾"
7,118 SF

35th- 40th FLOOR RESIDENTIAL
+ 729'-5 ¼"- 784'-0 ¾"
2,322 SF

34th FLOOR AMENITY LEVEL
+ 718'- 6 ¾"
3,189 SF

25th - 33rd FLOOR RESIDENTIAL
+ 620'- 3 ½"- 707'-7 ½"
4,852 SF

11th - 19th FLOOR RESIDENTIAL
+ 467'- 5 ¾"- 554'-9 ½"
3,325 SF

10th FLOOR AMENITY LEVEL
+ 456'-6 ¾"
3,428 SF

2nd - 9th FLOOR RESIDENTIAL
+ 369'-2 ½"- 445'-7 ½"
4,286 SF

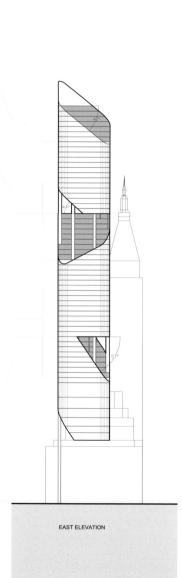

EAST ELEVATION

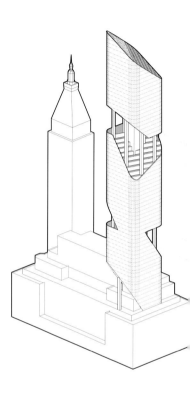

6.1

6 Layout and Presentation

In architectural design, layout and presentation form a critical part of the design process because the architect relies heavily on the successful representation of their ideas to convince the viewer of the feasibility of their scheme. The architect needs to create graphically seductive images that are both interesting and engaging, and describe the proposed scheme so well that the viewers can envisage themselves in this future space.

Appropriateness of the presentation type to the design concept needs to be carefully considered and balanced. Drawings such as plans, sections, and elevations explain a building in a measured and defined form. Other drawings can be more emotive and suggest an environment for, or an experience of, the architecture.

Minimal, modern building proposals are often described by minimal drawings that use simple lines and plain backgrounds; classically embellished building proposals will be described by crafted, decorated drawings. Appropriateness of presentation is determined by the drawing's relationship to the architectural style.

Layout is also part of the design process. Arranging or organizing drawings so that they tell the story of the architecture in a considered and coherent way is vital if the architect is to successfully communicate their design proposal. A "set" of architectural drawings (here, this term is used to imply the connection between individual drawings to describe the architecture as coherently as possible) must place the building in its physical and design context.

6.1

Project: New York Tower
Location: New York, USA
Architect: Studio Daniel Libeskind

The New York Tower project is part of a residential project for 1 Madison Avenue creating a new landmark on the skyline. The tower contains a series of gardens that spiral across the façade of the building, maximizing light and air for its residents.

These final presentation drawings show a series of diagrams examining the residential and garden floor areas in relation to sun angles. This information is also aligned to the elevation for the building. Linking the two together allows us to see how the gardens change throughout the tower. The key concepts are clearly communicated in diagrammatic form.

Layout

The layout of architectural images will affect the viewer's interpretation of a design concept. A set of plan, elevation, and section drawings can be arranged to create a 3D form of a building proposal, and the way in which these drawings are organized is important; arranged correctly, they tell the right story.

The plans serve as maps, explaining the relationships between rooms, spaces, and routes. The sections, when read in conjunction with the plans, explain the height of and vertical relationships between the building's spaces. The elevations explain the relationships between the doors and openings described in the plans. To tell the story of the architecture correctly, these drawings should be carefully presented so that their interrelationships are clearly evident.

Paper size

Many architectural drawings are created in CAD software programs that can produce images at any format and size. The decision of what size to render these images at will be determined to their printed format, which is in turn governed by where and how the work will be presented.

Larger formats (such as A0, A1 and A2 sheets) are useful for presentation drawings for an exhibition or public examination. The smaller A3 and A4 formats are quicker and cheaper to produce, but they are limited in the amount of information that they can communicate; there is only so much content that can be contained on these sheet sizes.

ISO paper sizes (plus rounded inch values)

Format A series

Size	mm x mm	in x in
A0	841 x 1189	33.1 x 46.8
A1	594 x 841	23.4 x 33.1
A2	420 x 594	16.5 x 23.4
A3	297 x 420	11.7 x 16.5
A4	210 x 297	8.3 x 11.7
A5	148 x 210	5.8 x 8.3
A6	105 x 148	4.1 x 5.8

Format B series

Size	mm x mm	in x in
B0	1000 x 1414	39.4 x 55.7
B1	707 x 1000	27.8 x 39.4
B2	500 x 707	19.7 x 27.8
B3	353 x 500	13.9 x 19.7
B4	250 x 353	9.8 x 13.9
B5	176 x 250	6.9 x 9.8
B6	125 x 176	4.9 x 6.9

Format C series

Size	mm x mm	in x in
C0	917 x 1297	36.1 x 51.1
C1	648 x 917	25.5 x 36.1
C2	458 x 648	18.0 x 25.5
C3	324 x 458	12.8 x 18.0
C4	229 x 324	9.0 x 12.8
C5	162 x 229	6.4 x 9.0
C6	114 x 162	4.5 x 6.4

Portrait or landscape?

Once the paper size has been determined, the orientation of the sheets needs to be decided upon.

Landscape format describes a horizontal orientation; portrait format describes a vertical one. This terminology finds its origins in the fine arts: landscape paintings (as the name suggests) often depicted landscape scenes and the horizon, whereas the tradition of portrait painting was characterized by depicting a human figure or a face within a vertical frame.

The choice of "frame" for architectural drawings will be influenced by similar factors. A building situated within the landscape, for example, will better relate to a horizontal frame, whereas plans for a skyscraper will sit better in a vertical frame.

Traditionally, all architectural drawings were displayed in landscape orientation. Drawings were produced on landscape boards and elevations were produced as horizontal strips that were linked to the building's plans, allowing a clear connection between the drawings on the sheet.

Nowadays, architectural drawings need to project a "possible reality"—real spaces that have possible functions, lifestyles, or experiences attached to them. In a sense, architectural drawings can be used as a form of advertising, projecting the architectural scheme as a lifestyle choice to the viewer. Very often these presentation drawings need to incorporate both the practical, measured architectural elements as well as exciting inspirational visuals.

ANSI paper sizes

In 1995, the American National Standards Institute (ANSI) adopted ANSI/ASME Y14.1, which defined a regular series of paper sizes. This series is somewhat similar to the ISO paper size standard in that cutting a sheet in half would produce two sheets of the next smaller size.

Name	in x in	mm x mm	Similar ISO size
ANSI A	8 x 11	279 x 216	A4
ANSI B	11 x 17	432 x 279	A3
ANSI C	17 x 22	559 x 432	A2
ANSI D	22 x 34	864 x 559	A1
ANSI E	34 x 44	1118 x 864	A0

In addition to the ANSI system, there is a corresponding series of paper sizes used for architectural purposes. This series also shares the property that bisecting each size produces two of the size below.

Name	in x in	mm x mm
Arch A	12 x 9	305 x 229
Arch B	18 x 12	457 x 305
Arch C	24 x 18	610 x 457
Arch D	36 x 24	914 x 610
Arch E	48 x 36	1219 x 914
Arch E1	42 x 30	1067 x 762

Organizing sets of drawings

The organization of measured drawings requires careful editing to ensure the clarity of their presentation. It is possible to have a set of drawings that incorporates several different scales; however, unless they are all absolutely necessary, it is usually better to limit the number of differently scaled images. For example, a location plan may be produced at 1:1250 in order to locate the position of the project in the context of its surrounding environment. This introduces one level of scale so it may then be simpler to ensure that the rest of the drawings are produced at a building scale of 1:200 (see page 37) so the viewer only has to read two or three levels across the whole presentation.

When assembling a range of drawings, it can be useful to sketch out the layout of each as a thumbnail image (a small, not-to-scale sketch) to highlight the relationships between each of the drawings and the information they contain. This can help plan the organisation and ensure that the scheme is communicated correctly and that the drawings complement one another.

Collectively, the drawings need to tell the story of the scheme. As such, concept images should be seen first to explain the origins of the architect's ideas. The location plan also needs to appear at an early stage as it describes where the building sits on a site. The site and ground plans should be read next, followed by any other building plans. The plans need to be adjacent to one another so that they can be read together, providing an explanation of the relationships between elements that work vertically within the building and across the scheme's floor plans. All plan drawings should be presented in the same orientation.

6.2
_____

Project: Orestad Church
Competition
Location: Orestad,
Copenhagen, Denmark
Designers: Joshua Kievenaar
and Natasha Butler

These competition presentation boards are carefully considered in terms of layout. The overall page is divided into three, with each drawing (perspective or section) being given equal priority. Each drawing has been selected as it summarizes the scheme and sells the idea. It works without further explanation or annotations.

6.2

Elevation drawings

Elevation drawings need to refer back to the plan drawings. Positioning the elevation drawings directly beneath their associated plan is helpful because it allows the viewer to read the connections between, say, the door and window openings on both drawings. Elevation drawing titles should reference their orientation (such as the south- or north-facing elevation), so one can immediately understand which part of the building receives most sunlight.

Any section drawing should clearly correspond to the position on the plan where its "cut" is taken. This should be indicated on the plan with the title of the section drawing (such as "Section AA" or "Section BB").

A good visual presentation should not be cluttered, it needs to have sufficient space to allow the information to be easily read and absorbed. The information may be rendered in varying sizes or use different graphic styles and techniques. The drawings must align purposefully as this will help the viewer read the drawings as a collective set.

6.3

**Project: Blackfriars Bridge
Location: London, UK
Architect: CJ Lim/Studio 8
Architects**

This collage mixes real images of Blackfriars Bridge with seaside themed visuals, such as ice cream vans, beach huts, and beach balls, combining an understood reality with an imagined fantasy.

The resulting imagined-reality image is powerful and provocative, suggesting a reinvention of the bridge.

Graphic presentations

The graphic presentation of architectural drawings should complement the design idea. There are many occasions where the presentation of a proposal relies solely on the graphic presentation (such as in examinations or for competition entries). As such, the presentation must clearly communicate the architect's idea, concept, and intention. To do so requires a balance between the information contained within the drawings and any supplementary text or visuals supporting them. Achieving this balance ensures that the layout of the building design and architectural features can be read easily and accurately.

The style of a graphic presentation can vary by the use of different colors, drawing techniques, sizes or types of imagery, and font sizes and styles. Some of these choices can be cleverly made so that the style of the graphic presentation echoes the style of the proposed architecture.

Measured drawings have a scale associated with them, so they need to be reproduced accurately. It should be remembered when composing an architectural presentation that as well as producing seductive graphics, the scheme has to be shown to work practically and functionally.

Imagined-reality visuals

Imagined-reality visuals are intended to excite and invigorate the viewer. They are impressions of a place or space created by the architect, and as such the use of color and the creation of a certain sense of drama are important considerations. The layout of a visual element must connect strongly to the content of the image. For example, there may be pictures of activities associated with the proposed architecture that can be included to unite the presentation and the underlying concept. These visuals may form the centerpiece to a series of measured drawings or create a theme for the presentation across a range of laid-out pages.

6.4

Project: Conceptual
Location: Havant, UK
Designers: Joshua Kievenaar and Natasha Butler

This model presentation sheet is organized around a grid, which has shaped its content and defines how we view the model images. Visual priority in the image is provided by colored or gray scale images and the area of the grid used. Text sections are identified with the use of colored squares, and these are linked to specific images with arrows.

6.4

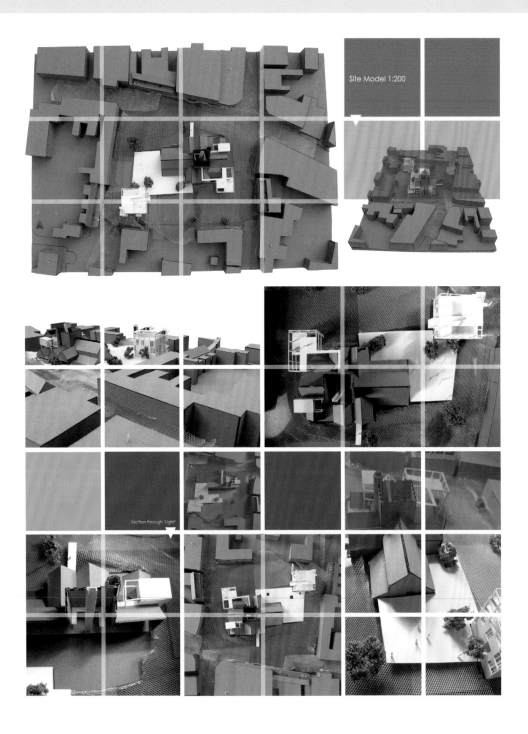

Site Model 1:200

Section through 'Light'

6.5

Supplementary text

The information contained within the presentation drawings can be supplemented by accompanying text. This text is another important element in the design of a graphic presentation, and its display needs to be carefully considered; for example, it might be boxed out or weaved into the actual drawings. Remember, however, that this text is supplementary; the drawings should remain the primary means of communication.

As with the choice of line weight for drawings, the style and size of the font will affect the viewer's interpretation of the supplementary text. The hierarchy of the text and how this relates to the drawings should be carefully considered.

The rules

A graphic presentation is usually a complex mix of different levels of information, composed of several drawings that are displayed on the same sheet. It is therefore vital to adhere to certain guidelines in order to ensure that all the levels of information and the different elements of content are read correctly.

All graphic presentations need a title. This may be the name of the building or the title of the project, but either way it should appear in a larger text size so it can be read from a distance. Each individual drawing needs to be labeled clearly so that the viewer can immediately distinguish the plans, sections, and elevations.

The scale of each drawing should also be clear. If several scales are used on one image, then it should be easy for the viewer to distinguish which images use which scale.

As the drawings become more detailed, the size of any text within them will become progressively smaller. To ensure that the information can still be viewed correctly, detailed drawings should use a numerical key or a legend, or incorporate symbols that allow the viewer to identify the different spaces or functions within the scheme.

6.5

Project: Conceptual
Location: Havant, UK
Designers: Joshua Kievenaar and Natasha Butler

This model presentation sheet uses a grid structure to organize its content and defines how we view the model images. Priority is drawn to certain images with their representation as colored or gray scale images. Text is identified by using colored squares and linked to specific images with arrows.

Oral presentations

Graphic presentations are often accompanied by an oral presentation, which is usually carried out by the architect or originator of the work. The oral presentation provides yet another opportunity to elaborate the concept underlying the scheme, explain the connections between the presentation images, and describe the idea of the scheme in further detail.

When presenting a scheme orally, connecting the commentary to each of the drawings is key. A good oral presentation (like a good graphic presentation) tells the story of the design process, from initial concept through to the development of the scheme's details. Key aspects of the concept should be outlined at the start of the presentation to identify the primary drivers in the scheme's development.

The rules

In schools of architecture, the oral presentation is called the "crit" (critique) or the design review. Oral presentations in professional practice (to a client) are referred to as a "pitch". Whether presenting to a client, colleagues, or examiners, it is vital to ensure that you know your audience and have addressed the parameters of the project brief for your scheme.

The oral presentation is an exercise in the promotion of your design and your opportunity to convince the audience that it is both exciting and viable. When explaining a scheme, it helps to refer to all the drawings, sketches, and models in your graphic presentation in order to fully describe how the building will be realized and how it might function. Doing so will convince your audience that you have explored all the design possibilities sensitively.

The oral presentation should be executed much like a piece of theater; it should be rehearsed, all the props (your drawings and models) should be present, and your audience should be engaged at all times.

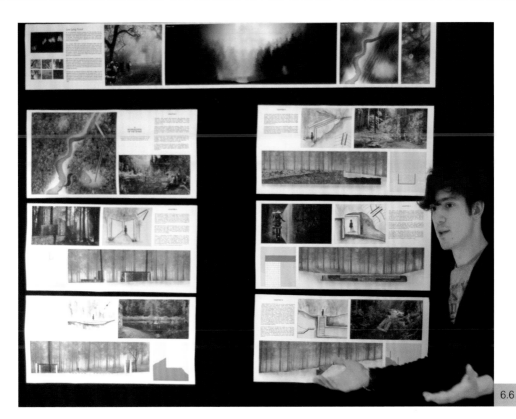

6.6

6.6

Presentation and exhibition

When presenting or exhibiting a proposed scheme, the images will form part of a story. Often, the architect or designer will orally describe the scheme, and this animates the images and brings together the different strands behind the concept. In doing so, the designer can reveal aspects of the idea that may not be apparent in the drawings and emphasize the important conceptual drivers for the project. Also, importantly, questions about a design can be answered directly.

Storyboards

Storyboarding is a technique often used by architects as a means to plan their concept or scheme. Much like a comic strip, storyboards are composed of frames that collectively explain how the architecture may be used or function over time. It applies a narrative to the design concept.

There are many ways for storyboards to be used as a successful presentation tool. They offer a means of describing and analyzing the uses and functions of buildings or spaces over time, which means that the architect (or viewer) can critically appraise the scheme. Storyboards can also be used to describe a series of potential views of a journey through the scheme, which can suggest how the building may be experienced over time.

Storyboards can be constructed from freehand sketches, measured drawings, or from a series of fly-through images that are organized sequentially. Physical models can also be photographed and presented as a series of stills within a storyboard frame.

The storyboard can also be a very helpful tool in the design development process because it can represent spatial sequence, which means that the architect can visualize and consider connected or associated spaces. Additionally, storyboards can be used as a helpful means of planning graphic presentations or offering an overview of the connections and relationships between the different visual elements of a presentation.

The frame is a useful element of the storyboard as it separates the drawings and can allow different viewpoints of the same form to be presented.

Showing a proposed structure three-dimensionally allows the viewer to see "around" the building form, which is particularly appropriate if the form is complex and multifaceted. Different views or aspects of a building form can be superimposed into a single presentation using framed boxes to highlight different elements of the scheme.

Storyboard for the Cube

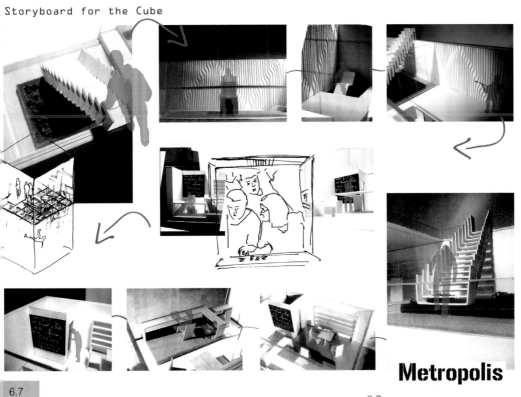

6.7

Metropolis

6.7

Project: Metropolis
Location: Conceptual
Designer: Aleksandra Wojciak

This storyboard explains
a design idea as a story.
The sheet is generated by
combining model photography
with sketches. Each image
describes how you move
through the sequence of
spaces; much like writing
a story, the design ideas
behind this project needed
to be described with a clear
beginning, middle, and end.

Portfolios

A portfolio contains representative samples of design work and can be produced in either a physical or electronic format (or a mixture of media). Producing a portfolio is a design exercise in itself. It needs to communicate ideas and information clearly through a considered narrative, careful organization and layout of information, and well-placed text and graphics.

The objectives of the portfolio

Like a graphic or oral presentation, understanding the needs of your portfolio's audience is the first step in its construction. Is it to be used to secure a job interview or a place on a course, or will it form part of a client pitch? The audience of your portfolio will affect both its content and its organization. For example, a portfolio compiled to secure a place on an academic course will have to meet pre-defined criteria and demonstrate your competence and aptitude as a potential student. Similarly, a portfolio produced for a job interview might display a range of work that echoes the style of your potential employer.

Defining the content, format and frame

Once the needs of the audience are established, the next step is to make a list of the drawings and images that need to be contained in the portfolio. A good portfolio will showcase a range of images, both freehand and computer generated, and from concept through to scheme details, to display different ideas across a range of media and representational techniques.

As with any presentation, the design of the images and their relationship to the format is key. It is useful to keep the format of all the portfolio's pages consistent. If this isn't possible, then try to group pages together so the viewer doesn't have to keep turning pages of the portfolio to view and understand the work.

Physical portfolios may be framed in a wallet or ring binder (which can create a series of pages, much like a book), or a plastic wallet (although these can sometimes create a barrier between the drawing and the viewer and should be used carefully). If the portfolio is created on CD, then the cover of the CD and the cover case itself can also be designed.

Interactive web-based portfolios are becoming more and more commonplace. The content, format, and frame of web portfolios are just as important as it is for physical ones. Online portfolios allow for a vast range of work to be displayed. Thumbnail images can be displayed on the site's home page and linked to their associated project images with information held elsewhere on the site, allowing the viewer to easily select and fully view the work of most interest to them.

SECTION 2 - 2 SCALE 1:50

ROOF DETAIL

BAY ELEVATION SCALE 1:50

PRIMARY, SECONDARY FRAME

ENVIRONMENTAL RESPONSE
SUN DIAGRAM

VENTILATION • HEATING • COOLING

6.8

6.8

Project: Design Center
Location: Conceptual
Designer: Aivita Mateika

Portfolio sheets—whether hard copy or digital files—need to be carefully compiled and edited. Much like writing a story, the building design needs to be carefully described with a clear beginning, middle, and end. This sheet uses a range of drawing types and hierarchies of information to ensure clear communication.

Case study: Crystals CityCenter, USA by Studio Daniel Libeskind

Presentation drawings

Studio Daniel Libeskind was commissioned by MGM Mirage to produce a new retail district called "Crystals" on the Las Vegas Strip, as part of their CityCenter master plan. The scheme aims to enliven the Strip and makes CityCenter an international destination. The retail area offers shopping, dining, and entertaining under one roof.

The concept of the scheme was a crystalline sculpture, which appears like fragments sitting in opposition to the surrounding more linear, vertical buildings. From every angle, "Crystals" appears as a work of art reflecting the city around it.

The different qualities of the interior and exterior enhance the form of the building as they contrast one another. The reflective, metal-clad roof draws pedestrians into the interior retail area designed by the Rockwell Group. Skylights within the roof's dramatic angles bathe the interior in natural light.

The design and construction of "Crystals" uses environmentally conscious practices and materials. It is the largest retail district to receive the Leadership in Energy and Environmental Design (LEED +) Core Gold and Shell Certification from the United States Green Building Council. The skin is made of stainless steel and glass, curtain-wall cladding. Each piece of cladding is unique, with no straight angles; approximately sixteen thousand components were needed.

The scheme uses a range of drawings to present the key ideas: from quick concept sketches capturing an idea to describe the relationship to the surrounding site and the bright lights of the Vegas Strip, to scale technical drawings communicating the complex sculptural form and containing the detail required for construction.

For this scheme, the architect's vision remains clear throughout the design process. For example, we can read the sculptural form in the fractured roofline represented within the section drawing and the detail design.

These initial sketch ideas are translated to a computer drawing to continue the design process. A digital drawing and modeling process allows for the detailing of the complex cladding forms. Large schemes such as this require a range of scales of engagement in terms of thinking and drawing.

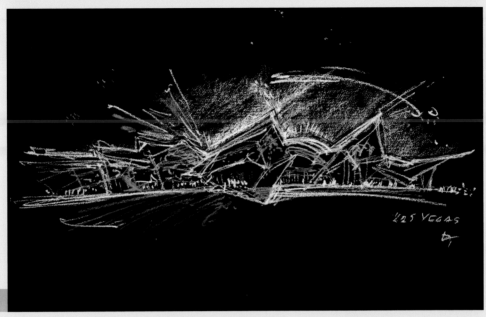

6.9a

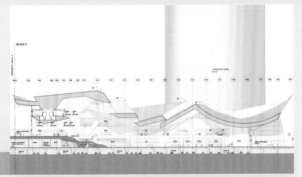

6.9b

6.9c

6.9a–6.9c

**Project: Crystals at CityCenter
Location: Las Vegas, USA
Architect: Studio Daniel
Libeskind**

Image 6.9a shows the dynamic
sketch for Crystals. The long
section (image 6.9b) cuts
through the main spaces of the
Crystals center and reveals
the interior spaces. It exposes
the overlapping roof forms and
shows how the skylights light
the interior.

The exterior photograph of
Crystals (image 6.9c) captures
the metal-clad crystalline forms.
The city sits as a backdrop
with the complex rooflines
contrasting with the linear lines
of the surrounding buildings.

Project: Planning presentation layouts

This student project uses the concept of regeneration in the Agrigento region on the southern coast of Sicily, Italy. The scheme aims to reinvent Agrigento, Italy as a food destination for tourists to get involved with the local produce.

The town of Agrigento is located on a steep hillside with challenging terrain, and the project aimed to identify spaces within the town for food production. The green spaces create a Landscape Park Green Boulevard, which connects public space together and becomes a meadow staircase. The final architectural piece introduces allotments and a cookery school.

This project illustrates how the method of storyboarding can be used to organize and plan a final presentation, exhibition, and portfolio. The information included should be clear and concise and ensure that no vital information is left out. The purpose of using a storyboard is to visualize how the narrative or story of the architectural idea will flow.

Process

Planning a portfolio needs careful consideration and organization, but using a storyboard framework can help you to organize the content of your portfolio.

Before you begin:

1 Determine the audience for your portfolio. What will they want to see?

2 Write an outline or brief for your portfolio.

3 Draw up a sequenced list of content (limit the number of pages or projects it will contain).

4 Consider the best format and layout of the pages.

5 Choose a font style and size that will complement your images. Remember you will need to use the font consistently throughout.

6 Consider the distinct sections of the portfolio (think of it like a book, there may be themes or projects that help to subdivide the portfolio's content).

Once these steps are complete, you are ready to map out a "flat plan"— a visual diagram or layout—of your portfolio's pages.

7 Use boxes or a series of frames to denote the imaginary pages of your portfolio. Indicate in words and sketches the sequence of projects and the specific images associated with each.

8 Label each page according to the sequenced list of contents you compiled earlier (see step 3).

9 Consider how the pages connect to one another. Edit and revise as necessary until you are happy with the narrative.

10 Once you are happy with the narrative, assemble your portfolio so that it corresponds with the flat plan.

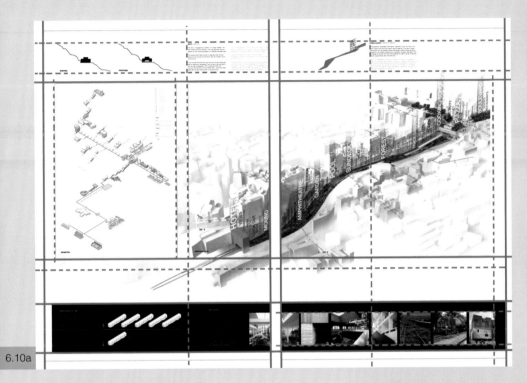

6.10a

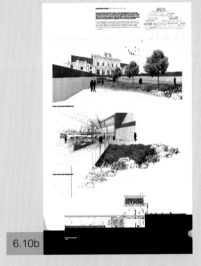

6.10b

6.10a–6.10b

Project: Final presentation and exhibition design
Designer: Dean Fitton and Graham Lake

These images illustrate a storyboard and how to organize a presentation or exhibition. The purpose of using a structure (grid or storyboard) is to visualize how work will flow and address your intended audience in the way that you want them to. A grid has been used to ensure alignment and priority of images.

Conclusion

Successful representation of an architectural scheme or concept presents a challenge. To be a success, the form of representation needs to communicate a range of concepts from a scheme's creative idea to its technical specifications.

To do this effectively, an understanding of the building's design is needed so that this can be translated in sketches, drawings, and models. How this design is communicated to the audience through the architect's chosen media, form of representation, and selection of layout and graphics allows architectural drawings to be ultimately variable.

Architectural drawings and models represent a future vision of a proposed building. Many of these proposals are never realized, yet architectural drawings possess a legitimate quality; the buildings they display could exist. As such, they are not images of something that is but something that could be; they need to have a persuasive power and to give confidence to their audience that the architecture could in fact be realized. The power of the architect is to stimulate the visual imagination through drawing.

The architect's drawing style must respond to these shifts; it needs to be culturally relevant and relate to the zeitgeist. It must reflect the changes in the surrounding cultural landscape around art, advertising, fashion, and marketing.

Plans and section drawings are specific devices that communicate architectural space and form, but beyond this, in the current climate of cross-disciplinary learning and teaching, architectural drawing has much to gain from its artistic neighbors in terms of rendering and representational techniques.

6.11a

Architectural representation can be a straightforward practical interpretation of a proposal; however, it ultimately needs to inspire—the possibilities of the space, building, or place need to be communicated to the audience. It may need a simple sketch or a complex computer model, but the designer must be ready and have the skills necessary to explain the possibility of the idea.

The relationship between the hand skills of drawing and the technical possibilities of the computer are interdependent and evolving to suggest new possibilities of thinking and making buildings.

6.11b

6.11c

6.11a – 6.11c

Project: Nam June Paik Museum
Location: Kyonggi, South Korea
Architect: CJ Lim/Studio 8 Architects

These CAD drawings are conceptual drawings that describe the architect's ideas as a sketch in plan. Of the concept, CJ Lim notes:

"The Nam June Paik Museum [is] nestled [within] the pine forest... the concept evolved through a simultaneous proliferation of graphite lines, planes, and ray-traced volumes. The butterfly wall is a visual metaphor for the white noise on an untuned television set, an unusual incidence of nature designed and constructed to mimic the electronic.

The images engage with the forms three-dimensionally and explore the lines and planes of the building as well as its relationship to the surrounding landscape. These engaging and exciting images are artworks in themselves. They describe a potential dynamic form engaged with a dramatic landscape."

Glossary

Aerial perspective
A constructed view of a building or site from above, this kind of view allows an understanding of the context of the site.

Axonometric
Also known as "planometric", this is a 3D projection that uses a plan of a building space or object and rotates it through 45 degrees. The plan is then projected vertically to create a 3D image. This is a quick and effective way to create a 3D impression of a building.

BIM
Building Information Modeling is a process of creating a 3D model of a building that is used to inform its design and construction by the design team and also remains as a virtual representation of a building when finished.

CAD
Computer-aided drafting, or design systems, is used by architects and students to develop and present their architectural ideas. The software can be applied in varying contexts. 2D plans are more effectively produced by some software packages. Others can create an impressive fly-through series of images. Specialized software can render or color images with realistic effects of materials, finishes and shadow.

Collage
This technique has been associated with painters such as Georges Braque and Pablo Picasso. It involves the assembly of fragments of images to create a new composite image.

Composition
When creating a presentation of architectural drawings, the composition of the images is important. A well-composed image means that the information has been organized effectively so it can be easily understood.

Conceptual sketches
A concept is the driving idea behind any architecture. The concept starts at the initial design stage of a project and carries through the project as it develops.

CPI (coordinated production information)
CPI is a system of communicating a range of scales for varying sets of information within architectural drawings.

Cutaway
A drawing technique that reveals an aspect of a building or interior space. The image has a section that is removed or "cut away" to expose the inside of a building. It can also be used to explain how a building is assembled or constructed.

Elevation
An elevation is the presentation of a face of a building or an interior wall. The elevation is designed through an understanding of the section and the plan.

Exploded drawing
An exploded drawing explains how a building is constructed or assembled. It deconstructs each element and component of the architecture and explains how they fit together.

Figure ground mapping
During the seventeenth century Giambattista Nolli created a mapping description of Rome that depicted buildings as solid form and spaces as blank or empty areas. Figure ground maps provide a quick understanding of a city and its density. This technique is used in a variety of contexts from urban analysis to spatial interpretation.

Fly-through
CAD modeling has facilities that allow an architectural idea to be presented as a series of images to suggest a journey through a building or space. This series of images (or fly-through) can be composed as an animated film as if the viewer is "flying through" the space.

Isometric
This is a 3D projection that uses a plan of a building space or object and distorts it through 30 degrees. The plan is then projected vertically to create a 3D image.

Juxtaposition
When placing drawings adjacent to one another, there may be a sense of intentionally creating contrast of an idea or concept. Drawings of different scale can be juxtaposed in the same presentation.

Layout

This refers to the positioning of images, drawings and text on a page. Layout is a critical consideration for the understanding of a scheme.

Legend

Drawings use codes and symbols as a form of shorthand. This shorthand is a legend, which not only displays all the symbols used in the drawings but also explains their associated meanings. There are standard conventions and codes that are used to describe materials, fixtures and fittings.

Location plan

To initially understand a building or site proposal, a location plan is needed. This identifies the site for the proposal and its immediate context. It will "locates" the building and describes orientation and surrounding buildings and features.

Maquette

This is a small-scale model that represents and tests an architectural idea. A maquette can also be described as a sketch model or developmental model.

Orientation

Orientation is one of the ways in which a building relates to its site. It is described using the north point on the plan as a point of reference. Orientation refers to its relationship to the prevailing local climatic conditions such as the sun and the wind.

Parti

This is a type of drawing that reduces a concept of a building or scheme to its most simplified form so that it is easy to understand. Even the most complex building can be represented using a parti diagram. This is normally developed at the early stages of design and is a reference as the design evolves.

Perspective

This refers to the 2D representation or description of a 3D form or space.

Photomontage

This is a technique that merges one image of a building or object into another. CAD software allows for this type of image to be created quickly and effectively by merging digital photos or images.

Portfolio

A portfolio is a collection of information types. This can be comprised of drawings, photos, sketches, or computer animations. A portfolio is usually directed towards a particular audience or a particular project.

Proportion

This refers to the satisfactory relationship of individual parts to the whole. In architectural terms, proportion can apply to the idea of a building design or to the idea of a presentation drawing. The overall presentation needs to be proportionally correct in terms of organization and layout.

Render

A drawing may need additional color or texture finish to describe materials or color. Applying color or texture to a drawing is known as rendering.

Section

A section drawing is a vertical cut through a building or space. This cut reveals connections within the building between different floor levels, such as double height spaces or changes of level. Section drawings can also connect to the outside.

Sectional perspective

This is a hybrid drawing combining a perspective drawing with a section drawing. This can suggest a relationship occurring inside the building and connect it with one outside the building. A sectional perspective turns a 2Dl section into a 3D perspective drawing.

Storyboard

A storyboard is a visual framework that is used in many areas of design and graphic representation, from advertising to film-making. It can be a useful mechanism that explains a concept as a series of images (a bit like a comic strip). Storyboards can suggest both time and visual description.

Superimposition

Images may be used collectively to describe an idea. Superimposed images are layered on top of one another to create a composite picture.

Further resources

The following books, websites, organizations and resources can be used as a platform for further exploring representational techniques in architecture.

Bibliography

Ambrose, G and **Harris, P**
Basics Design: Layout
AVA Publishing SA, 2006

Ambrose, G and **Harris, P**
The Visual Dictionary of Architecture
AVA Publishing SA, 2006

Ching, FDK
Architectural Graphics
John Wiley & Sons, 2003

Coop, D
Drawing and Perceiving: Real-world Drawing for Students of Architecture and Design
John Wiley & Sons, 2007

Dawson, S
Architects Working Details (Number 10)
Emap Construct, 2004

Doyle, ME
Color Drawing: Design Drawing Skills and Techniques for Architects, Landscape Architects and Interior Designers
John Wiley & Sons, 1999

Dubery, F and **Williats, J**
Perspective and Other Drawing Systems
Von Nostrand Reinhold, 1983

Gombrich, EH
Art and Illusion
Phaidon Press, 1987

Laseau, P
Freehand Sketching: An Introduction
W.W. Norton & Company, 2004

Lim, CJ/Studio 8 Architects
Sins and Other Spatial Narratives
Studio 8 Architects, 2000

Linton, H
Portfolio Design (Third Edition)
W.W. Norton & Company, 2003

Maranovic, I, Ruedi Ray, K and **Lokko, L**
The Portfolio: An Architecture Student's Handbook
Architectural Press, 2004

Mills, CB
Designing with Models
John Wiley & Sons, 2005

Mitton, M
Interior Design Visual Presentation: A Guide to Graphics, Models, and Presentation Techniques
John Wiley & Sons, 2003

Porter, T and **Neale, J**
Architectural Supermodels: Physical Design and Simulation
Architectural Press, 2000

Reekie, RF
Reekie's Architectural Drawing
Architectural Press, 1995

Ruskin, J
The Elements of Drawing
The Herbert Press, 1987

Schank Smith, K
Architects' Drawings
Architectural Press, 2005

Styles, K
Working Drawings Handbook
Architectural Press, 2004

Materials and tools

4D Modelshop
www.modelshop.co.uk

EMA Model Supplies Ltd
www.ema-models.com

Imadethat3d
address
info@imadethat3d.com

Modulor
www.modulor.de

Mutr
www.mindsetsonline.co.uk

Squires Model and Craft Tools
www.squirestools.com

Software

www.archicad.com
This software has very useful 3D capabilities, and has a facility to create quick fly-through images. Also has a rendering package to create impressive 3D visuals.

www.googleearth.com
Software that connects to photographic maps of the world, which can be zoomed in and out to different scales.

www.photoshopsupport.com
Photoshop tutorials to give basic introduction to using Photoshop software.

www.sketchup.com
SketchUp is a 3D modeling software that can be used to quickly create basic models using plan information.

www.vectorworks.com
Vectorworks is a relatively easy-to-use software, initially used as a 2D drawing tool, which now also has 3D facilities.

Images

www.archinet.co.uk
A resource-based website that
provides good links to a range
of other architecture resources.

www.gettyimages.com
Images can be downloaded
from this site for use as
graphics to complement
architectural drawings.

www.riba.pix.com
Part of the Royal Institute of
British Architects, this site has
a picture library with a search
engine of a large range of
architectural images.

Practice

www.aia.org
The American Institute of
Architects website provides
advice and information on all
aspects of American architectural
education and practice.

www.architecture.com
A useful information site run by
the RIBA that provides details
about where to study in the UK
and links to other practice and
education sites.

www.eaae.be
EAAE is the European
Architectural Association
of Europe. Their site has
information about where to
study in Europe, and offers
details about a range of courses
and student competitions.

www.uia-architectes.org
The International Union of
Architects website has
connections all over the
world to professional and
educational websites.

Contributors

CJ Lim/Studio 8 Architects
www.cjlim-studio8.com

Coop Himmelb(l)au
www.coop-himmelblau.at

Design Engine Architects
www.designengine.co.uk

Dixon Jones Limited
www.dixonjones.co.uk

dRMM Architects
www.drmm.co.uk

Foster + Partners
www.fosterandpartners.com

HOK Architects
www.hok.com

Hyde + Hyde Architects
www.hydearchitects.com

John Pardey Architects
www.johnpardeyarchitects.com

Morphosis Architects
www.morphosis.net

PAD Studio
www.padstudio.co.uk

Piercy & Company Architects
www.piercyconner.co.uk

Pierre d'Avoine Architects
www.davoine.net

S333 Architecture + Urbanism
www.s333.org

Sean Godsell Architects
www.seangodsell.com

Steven Holl Architects
www.stevenholl.com

Studio Daniel Libeskind
www.daniel-libeskind.com

Index

Acknowledgements

This book could not have been realized without the personal and professional support, encouragement, contributions, and efforts received from a range of individuals.

Thanks are owed to the many architectural practices that have taken time to contribute their images and drawings to this book. A book about architectural representation can only be realized if architects are prepared to share their ideas and approaches to architectural drawing. Architects have traditionally learned through this altruistic approach to teaching and learning, and this spirit does still exist.

With this in mind we would like to offer special thanks to:

CJ Lim/Studio 8 Architects, Design Engine Architects, Foster & Partners, HOK Architects, Kristian Hyde at Hyde + Hyde Architects, PAD Studio, Steven Holl Architects, Gregory Martínez de Riquelme, Sean Godsell Architects, and Studio Daniel Libeskind.

Thanks are also due to The School of Architecture, University of Portsmouth 2013/2014. With special thanks to Bruna Fleck and Ioaniss Miltiadou, students who helped with the organization and picture research for the book; Kate Duffy as editor who supported the book throughout its evolution, and to Jane Harper for the book's design.

Personally, thanks to our partners, family, and friends for their patience and understanding over the last year.

Picture credits

The publishers would like to thank the following contributors for allowing us to use their work:

Adam Parsons pp 20–1, 86–7, 104–5; Aleksandra Wojciak pp 69, 169; Aivita Mateika pp 42–3, 51, 112–3, 126–7, 171; Bruna Fleck and Ioannis Miltiadou p153; CJ Lim/Studio 8 Architects pp 39, 107, 115, 117, 119, 160–1, 176–7; Extracted from documents provided by Coop Himmelb(l)au pp 61, 143, 150–1; Darren Leach pp 121; Dave Holden p44; David Yearly, Lorraine Farrelly, Matt Mardell, Alex Wood and Architecture PLB pp 48–9; Dean Fitton and Graham Lake pp 122, 175; Design Engine Architects Ltd pp 12–3, 90, 139–141; Dixon Jones p18; dRMM pp 46–7, 64–5; © Foster + Partners p67 photo courtesy Nigel Young; Hampshire County Architects Property Services pp 146–7; © HOK p95 photo courtesy Moris Moreno; Hyde & Hyde Architects p70; Group Design p50; Jeremy Davies pp 28–9, 53, 103; Joshua Kievenaar p11 and Natasha Butler pp 78–9, 88, 159, 163–4; John Pardey Architects pp 73, 84, 92–3; Jonny Sage p8; Khalid Saleh pp 60, 148–9; Lorraine Farrelly p33; Marcus Pillhofer pp 150–1; Metropolitan Workshop p111; courtesy of Morphosis Architects p34; Nathan Fairbrother, University of Portsmouth p27; Niall C Bird pp 19, 24–5; Nicholas Surtees pp 22–3; Nicola Crowson pp 69, 81, 101, 104, 167; 2011, Nora Pucher and Christoph Zechmeister p137; PAD Studio pp 17, 125; Paul Cashin p109 and Simon Drayson p97; Piercy & Company London Ltd p98; Pierre d'Avoine Architects pp 62–3; RBA Architects p145; courtesy of Ricardo Marques p131; Robert Cox pp 36, 54–5; Dominic Papa & Jonathan Woodroffe at S333 Architecture + Urbanism pp 56–7; Sean Godsell Architects p31; Sir Colin Stansfield Smith and John Pardey p85; Sophie Bellows p59; Steven Holl Architects pp 14–15, 41, 75–7, 80–3, 100–01, 134–5; Studio Daniel Libeskind pp 3, 132, 154, 173 photo courtesy S. Frances; Toby Richardson and Sam Sclater-Brooks pp 102, 128.